RICK JOYNER

MorningStar Publications

A DIVISION OF MORNINGSTAR FELLOWSHIP CHURCH

375 Star Light Drive, Fort Mill, SC 29715

The Final Quest
by Rick Joyner
Copyright © 1996
Mass Market Edition
11th Printing, 2016

Distributed by MorningStar Publications, Inc.,
a division of MorningStar Fellowship Church
375 Star Light Drive, Fort Mill, SC 29715
www.MorningStarMinistries.org
1-800-542-0278

International Standard Book Number—978-1-929371-90-7; 1-929371-90-X

Cover Design: Kevin Lepp
Book Layout: Dana Zondory

Unless otherwise indicated, all Scripture quotations are taken from the New American Standard Bible, copyright © 1960, 1962, 1963, 1968, 1971, 1973, 1974, 1977 by The Lockman Foundation. Italics in Scripture are for emphasis only.

Table of Contents

INTRODUCTION

This book stems from an extraordinary dream I had in early 1995. I published a condensed version of the first dream in *The MorningStar Prophetic Bulletin* and *The Morning Star Journal* under the title, "The Hordes of Hell Are Marching." As I continued to seek the Lord about this great spiritual battle that I had seen, I received a series of related visions and prophetic experiences. Condensed versions of these were published in *The Morning Star Journal* as "The Hordes of Hell Are Marching, Parts II and III."

The articles in this series became the most popular writings I have ever published. We were deluged with requests to have all of the parts published together in a book. I determined to do this and set out to fill in all that had been left out of the condensed versions. However, just when I was ready to give this to our editing department, I had another prophetic experience that was obviously related to this vision, containing what I felt were the most important parts of all. These are included in Parts IV and V of this book.

How I Received the Vision

This is the most common question I receive about this vision, so I will attempt to briefly answer it here. First, I must explain what I mean by visions and "prophetic experiences."

Prophetic experiences are numerous and diverse and include all of the primary ways that God spoke to His people in the Scriptures. Because the Lord is the same today as He was yesterday, He has never ceased to speak to His people in the same ways, which we see continued in the New Testament just as in the Old. The same supernatural experiences found in the Scriptures can be seen throughout church history and are becoming increasingly common today. In the sermon by the Apostle Peter recorded in Acts 2:14-21, he explains that dreams, visions, and prophecy are primary signs of the outpouring of the Holy Spirit in the last days. Since we are obviously coming closer to the end of this age, these signs are therefore becoming increasingly common with Christians.

One reason why experiences such as dreams, visions, and prophecy are becoming so much more common now is because we will need them for accomplishing our purposes in these times. It is also true that Satan, who unfortunately knows the Scriptures better than many Christians, understands the importance of prophetic revelation in God's relationship with His people. Satan is therefore pouring out his own counterfeit gifts in great measure to those who serve him. However, there would be no counterfeit if there was not a genuine reality, just as there are no counterfeit three-dollar bills because there are no real ones.

Soon after I became a Christian in 1972, I read Peter's sermon in Acts chapter two and realized that if we were in the end times, it was important to understand the ways that the Lord speaks to us. I do not remember praying at first to have the experiences myself, but I did begin having them, which gave me an even greater impetus for understanding them that I continue to pursue.

Since that time, I have gone through periods when prophetic experiences were very frequent. I have also gone through long periods of time when I did not have any such experiences. Yet after each period of not having them, they returned, and were either much more powerful or much more frequent. Through all of this I have learned a great deal about prophetic gifts and prophetic people, and I have addressed the full scope of the prophetic ministry in my book, *The Prophetic Ministry*.

Different Levels of Revelation

There are many levels of prophetic revelation. The initial level is prophetic "impressions." These are genuine revelations or guidance from the Holy Spirit and a primary way that He speaks to believers. They can be extraordinarily specific and accurate when interpreted by those who are experienced and sensitive to them. However, on this level, our "revelations" can be affected by our own feelings, prejudices, and doctrines. I have therefore resolved not to use expressions such as "thus says the Lord" with any revelations that come on this level.

Visions can also come on the impression level. They are gentle and must be seen with "the eyes of our hearts." These, too, can be very specific and accurate, especially when received and/or interpreted by those who are experienced. The more the eyes of our hearts are opened, as Paul prayed in Ephesians 1:18, the more powerful and useful these can be.

The next level of revelation is a conscious sense of the presence of the Lord, or the anointing of the Holy Spirit, which gives special illumination to our minds. This often comes when I am writing or speaking, and it gives me much greater confidence in the importance or accuracy of what I am saying. However, while we may be emboldened by this sense of God's presence, we need to realize that this is still a level where we can be influenced by our pre-existing viewpoints and attitudes. I believe this is why, in certain matters, Paul would say he was giving his *opinion*, but that he *thought* he had the agreement of the Spirit of the Lord (see I Corinthians 7:40). In general, we need humility rather than dogmatism when we deal with the prophetic.

"Open visions" occur on a higher level than impressions, and they tend to give us even more clarity than we feel with the presence of the Lord or the anointing. Open visions are external and are like watching a movie screen. Since they cannot be controlled by us, there is far less possibility of mixture in revelations that come this way.

Another higher-level prophetic experience is a trance, which is like dreaming when you are awake. Instead of just seeing a "screen" like in an open vision, you feel as if you are *in* the movie—actually *there* in some strange way. Peter fell into a trance in Acts 10:10, when he was instructed to go to the house of Cornelius and preach the gospel to the Gentiles for the first time. Paul, likewise, refers in Acts 22:17 to a trance he experienced while praying in the temple.

Trances were common experiences among the biblical prophets. The depth of trances can range from being rather mild—so that you are still conscious of your physical surroundings and can even still interact with them—to feeling as if you are literally in the place of your vision. This seems to be what Ezekiel experienced rather frequently, and what John probably experienced when he had the visions recorded in the Book of Revelation.

The visions contained in this book all began with dreams. Dreams can also be a powerful level of revelation as it is hard for us to control our dreams. However, this is not to imply that our dreams cannot be influenced by what we are occupied with, or even what we ate before we went to sleep. However, prophetic dreams are unmistakably different. If you have to ask what that difference is you probably have not had one. It is unmistakable, but it is also hard to explain, just as it is hard for me to explain my wife's voice, but I know it instantly when I hear it. Dreams from God also have that same unmistakable quality so that you know they are from Him.

Some of these visions also came under a very intense sense of the presence of the Lord, but the majority were received in some level of a trance. Usually the visions came on a level where I was still conscious of my surroundings and could even interact with them, such as answering the phone. When the visions were interrupted, or when things got so intense I had to get up and walk around, they would immediately continue once I sat down again. One time the experience became so intense that I actually got up and left the mountain cabin where I had gone to seek the Lord and drove home. Over a week later, I returned and almost immediately was right back where I left off in the experience.

I have never known how to "turn on" such experiences, but I have almost always had the liberty to turn them off at will. Twice, large portions of this vision came at what I considered to be very inconvenient times, when I had gone to my cabin to get some important work done while facing deadlines. Two issues of *The Morning Star Journal* were a little late being published because of this, and one of my books was delayed a few months from when I had hoped to finish it. However, the Lord does not seem to be very concerned about our deadlines!

In the dreams and the trances, I had what I consider to be greatly magnified gifts of discernment and words of knowledge. Sometimes when I look at a person or pray for a church or ministry, I start to know things about them of which I have no natural knowledge. During the prophetic experiences recorded in this book, these gifts were operating on a level that I have never personally experienced in "real

life." For example, in this vision I could look at a div...
of the evil horde and immediately know all of its strategies
and capabilities.

I do not know how this enhanced knowledge came to
me, but I just knew it, and in great detail. At times I would
look at things or people and know their past, present, and
future all at once. To save time and space in this book, I
have included this knowledge as a matter of fact, without
going into an explanation of how I received it.

Using Prophetic Revelations

I must state emphatically that I do not believe that any
kind of prophetic revelation is for the purpose of establishing
doctrine. We have the Scriptures for that. There are two
basic uses for the prophetic. The first is for revealing the
present or future strategic will of the Lord in certain
matters. We have examples of this in Paul's dream to go
to Macedonia (see Acts 16:6-10) and in the trance where
he was told to quickly leave Jerusalem (see Acts 22:17-18).
We also have examples of this in the ministry of Agabus.
One of these concerned a famine that was coming upon the
whole world (see Acts 11:27-30), and the other had to do
with Paul's visit to Jerusalem (see Acts 21:10-12).

Such revelations are also given for illuminating doctrine
that is taught in the Scripture, but may not have been clearly
understood yet. For example, Peter's trance in Acts 10 not
only illuminated God's will for Peter, it also provided timely
insight on a matter in which Scriptures were very clear (the
Gentiles being able to receive the gospel), but which had
not yet been understood by the church.

While the visions in this book do contain some strategic revelations, they also shed light on some biblical doctrines that I honestly had not seen before, but now see quite clearly. However, for years I had known and taught most of the truths illuminated to me in these experiences, even though I cannot say that I had lived them all very well. Many times I thought about the warning Paul gave Timothy—to pay attention to his own teachings (see I Timothy 4:16). Confronted by my failure to live up to some of my own teachings, I therefore accepted many of these messages as a personal rebuke. Even so, I also felt they were general messages to the body of Christ, and so I included them here.

Some of my friends encouraged me to write this as an allegory, in the third person, like *The Pilgrim's Progress*. I decided against that for several reasons. First, I feel that some would have taken this to be the result of my own creativity, which would have been wrong. I would like to be this creative, but I am not.

I also felt I could be much more accurate if I related these experiences just as I received them, and I endeavored to do so. However, I consider my memory of details to be one of my greatest weaknesses. At times, I have questioned my memory about certain details in this vision, and you should therefore have the liberty to question some of them too. I think such scrutiny is wise with any such messages. Only the Scriptures deserve to be considered infallible. As you consider these experiences, I pray that the Holy Spirit will lead you to the truth and separate any chaff that may be present from the wheat.

Rick Joyner

The Final Quest

Part I

THE HORDES
OF HELL
ARE MARCHING

The demonic army was so large that it stretched as far as I could see. It was separated into divisions, with each carrying a different banner. The foremost divisions marched under the banners of Pride, Self-Righteousness, Respectability, Selfish Ambition, Unrighteous Judgment, and Jealousy. There were many more of these evil divisions beyond my scope of vision, but those in the vanguard of this terrible horde from hell seemed to be the most powerful. The leader of this army was the Accuser of the Brethren himself.

The weapons carried by this horde were also named. The swords were named Intimidation; the spears were named Treachery; and the arrows were named Accusation, Gossip, Slander, and Faultfinding. Scouts and smaller companies of demons with such names as Rejection, Bitterness, Impatience, Unforgiveness, and Lust were sent in advance of this army to prepare for the main attack.

These smaller companies and scouts were much fewer in number, but they were no less powerful than some of the larger divisions that followed. They were smaller only for strategic reasons. Just as John the Baptist was given an extraordinary anointing for baptizing the masses to prepare them for the Lord, these smaller demonic companies were given extraordinary evil powers for "baptizing the masses."

A single demon of Bitterness could sow his poison into multitudes of people, even entire races or cultures. A demon of Lust would attach himself to a single performer, movie, or advertisement and send what appeared to be bolts of electric slime that would hit and "desensitize" great masses of people. All of this was to prepare for the great horde of evil which followed.

Although this army was marching specifically against the church, it also was attacking anyone else that it could. I knew it was seeking to preempt a coming move of God, which was destined to sweep great numbers of people into the church.

The primary strategy of this army was to cause division on every possible level of relationship—churches with each other, congregations with their pastors, husbands and wives, children and parents, and even children with each other. The scouts were sent to locate the openings in churches, families, or individuals that such spirits as Rejection, Bitterness, and Lust could exploit and enlarge. Through these openings would pour demonic influences that completely overwhelmed their victims.

On the Backs of Christians

The most shocking part of this vision was that this horde was not riding on horses, but primarily on Christians!

Most of them were well-dressed, respectable, and had the appearance of being refined and educated, but there also seemed to be representatives from almost every walk of life. While these people professed Christian truths in order to appease their consciences, they lived their lives in agreement with the powers of darkness. As they agreed with those powers, their assigned demons grew and more easily directed their actions.

Many of these believers were host to more than one demon, but one of the demons would clearly be in charge. The nature of the one in charge dictated which division it was marching in. Even though the divisions were all marching together, it also seemed that the entire army was on the verge of chaos. For example, the demons of Hate hated the other demons as much as they did the Christians. The demons of Jealousy were all jealous of one another.

The only way the leaders of this horde kept the demons from fighting each other was to keep their hatred focused on the people they were riding. However, these people would often break out in fights with each other. I knew that some of the armies which came against Israel in the Scriptures had ended up destroying themselves in this same way. When their purpose against Israel was thwarted, their rage was uncontrollable, and they began fighting each other.

I noted that the demons were riding on Christians, but were not in them as was the case with non-Christians. It was obvious that these believers had only to stop agreeing with their demons in order to get free of them. For example, if the Christian on whom a demon of Jealousy was riding just started to question the jealousy, that demon would weaken very fast. When this happened, the weakened demon would cry out and the leader of the division would direct all the demons around that Christian to attack him until the jealousy would build up on him again. If this did not work, the demons would begin quoting Scriptures, perverting them in a way that would justify the bitterness, accusations, or other satanic influences they were spreading.

The power of the demons was clearly rooted almost entirely in the power of deception. However, they had deceived these Christians to the point where they could use them, and the Christians would think they were being used by God. This was because banners of Self-Righteousness were being carried by almost everyone, so that those marching could not even see the banners that marked the true nature of these divisions.

As I looked far to the rear of this army, I saw the entourage of the Accuser himself. I began to understand his strategy, and I was amazed that it was so simple. He knew that a house divided could not stand, and his army represented an attempt to bring such division to the church so that she would be powerless and ineffective.

It was apparent that the only way the Accuser could accomplish this was to use Christians to war against their own brethren, and that is why almost everyone in the forward divisions was a Christian, or at least a professing Christian. Every step these deceived believers took in obedience to the Accuser strengthened his power over them. This made his confidence and the confidence of all his commanders grow with the progress of the army as it marched forward. It was apparent that the power of this army depended on the agreement of these Christians with the ways of evil.

The Prisoners

Trailing behind these first divisions was a multitude of other Christians who were prisoners of this army. All of these captive Christians were wounded, and they were guarded by smaller demons of Fear. There seemed to be more prisoners than there were demons in the army.

Surprisingly, these prisoners still had their swords and shields, but they did not use them. It was a shock to see that so many could be kept captive by so few of the little demons of Fear. If the Christians had just used their weapons, they could easily have freed themselves and probably done great damage to the entire evil horde. Instead, they marched along submissively.

Above the prisoners, the sky was black with vultures named Depression. Occasionally, these vultures would land on the shoulders of a prisoner and vomit on him. The vomit was Condemnation. When the vomit hit a prisoner he would stand up and march a little straighter for a while, and then slump over, even weaker than before. Again, I wondered why the prisoners did not simply kill these vultures with their swords, which they could have easily done.

Sometimes the weaker prisoners would stumble and fall. As soon as they hit the ground, the other prisoners would begin stabbing them with their swords, scorning them for their weakness. The vultures would then come and begin devouring the fallen ones even before they were dead. The other Christian prisoners stood by and watched this approvingly, occasionally stabbing the fallen ones again with their swords.

As I watched, I realized that these prisoners thought the vomit of Condemnation was truth from God. Then I understood that these prisoners actually thought they were marching in the army of God! This is why they did not kill the little demons of Fear or the vultures—they thought these were God's messengers! The darkness from the cloud of vultures made it so hard for these prisoners to see that they naively accepted everything that happened to them as being from the Lord. They felt that those who stumbled were under God's judgment, which is why they attacked them the way they did—they thought they were helping God!

The only food provided for these prisoners was the vomit from the vultures. Those who refused to eat it simply weakened until they fell. Those who did eat it were strengthened for a time, but with the strength of the evil one. Then they would weaken unless they drank the waters of bitterness that were constantly being offered to them. After drinking the bitter waters, they would begin to vomit on the others. When one of the prisoners began to do this, a demon that was waiting for a ride would climb up on him and ride him up to one of the front divisions.

Satanic Slime

Even worse than the vomit from the vultures was a repulsive slime that these demons were urinating and defecating upon the Christians they rode. This slime was the pride, selfish ambition, etc., which was the nature of their division. However, this slime made the Christians feel so much better than the condemnation had that they easily believed the demons were messengers of God. They actually thought this slime was the anointing of the Holy Spirit.

I had been so repulsed by the evil army that I wanted to die. Then the voice of the Lord came to me saying, *"This is the beginning of the enemy's last-day army. This is Satan's ultimate deception. His greatest power of destruction is released when he uses Christians to attack one another. Throughout the ages he has used this army, but never has he been able to use so many for his evil purposes as he is now. Do not fear. I have an army, too. You must now stand and fight because there is no longer any place to hide from this war. You must fight for My kingdom, for truth, and for those who have been deceived."*

This word from the Lord was so encouraging that I immediately began yelling to the Christian prisoners that they were deceived, thinking they would listen to me. When I did this, it seemed that the whole army turned to look at me. The cloud of fear and depression that was over them started to come toward me.

I still kept yelling because I thought the Christians would wake up and realize what was happening to them. Instead, many of them started reaching for their arrows to shoot at me. The others just hesitated, as if they did not know what to make of me. I knew I had spoken out prematurely and that it had been a very foolish mistake.

The Battle Begins

Then I turned and saw the army of the Lord standing behind me. There were thousands of soldiers, but they were still greatly outnumbered. I was shocked and disheartened, for it seemed there were actually many more Christians being used by the evil one than there were in the army of the Lord. I knew that the battle that was about to begin was going to be viewed as the Great Christian Civil War because very few would understand the dark powers that were behind the impending conflict.

As I looked more closely at the army of the Lord, the situation seemed even more discouraging. Only a small number were fully dressed in their armor. Many only had one or two pieces of their armor on; some did not have any at all. A large number were already wounded. Most of those who had all their armor still had very small shields, which I knew would not protect them from the onslaught that was coming. Very few of those who were fully armed were adequately trained to use their weapons. To my further surprise, the great majority of these soldiers were women and children.

Behind this army was a trailing mob, which seemed very different in nature from the prisoners who followed the evil horde. Those in the mob seemed overly happy, as if intoxicated. They were playing games and singing songs, feasting, and roaming about from one little camp to the next. This reminded me of Woodstock.

I ran toward the army of the Lord to escape the onslaught I knew would be coming at me from the evil horde. In every way, it seemed we were in for a mostly one-sided slaughter. I was especially concerned for the mob that was trailing the Lord's army, so I tried to raise my voice above the clamor to warn them that a battle was about to begin. Only a few could even hear me. Those who heard gave me the "peace sign" and said they did not believe in war.

When those in the mob assured me that the Lord would not let anything bad happen to them, I tried to explain that He had given us armor because we needed it for what was about to take place. To this they retorted that they had come to a place of peace and joy where nothing like that could happen to them. I began praying earnestly for the Lord to increase the shields of those with the armor and to help protect those who were not ready for the battle.

Then a messenger came up to me, gave me a trumpet, and told me to blow it quickly. When I did, those who had at least some of their armor on immediately responded, snapping to attention. More armor was brought to them, which they quickly put on. I noticed that those who were wounded did not put armor over their wounds. Before I could say anything about this, enemy arrows began raining down on us. Those who did not have all of their armor on were wounded. Those who had not covered their wounds were struck again in the same wound.

Those who were hit by arrows of Slander immediately began to slander those who were not wounded. Those who were hit with Gossip began to gossip, and soon a major division had been created within our own camp. I felt that we were on the verge of destroying ourselves, just as some of the heathen armies in Scripture had done by rising up to kill each other. The feeling of helplessness was terrible.

The Vultures Appear

Then vultures swooped down to pick up the wounded and deliver them into the camp of prisoners. The wounded still had swords and could have easily struck down the vultures, but they did not. They were actually carried off willingly because they were so angry at those who were not wounded like they were.

I quickly thought about the mob behind the army and ran to see what had happened to them. It seemed impossible, but the scene among them was even worse. Thousands lay on the ground, wounded and groaning. The sky over them was darkened by the vultures that were carrying them off to become prisoners of the enemy.

Many of those who were not wounded just sat in a stupor of unbelief. They, too, were easily carried away by the vultures. Even though a few had begun trying to fight off the vultures, since they did not have the proper weapons, the vultures did not pay them any attention. The wounded were so angry they would threaten and drive away anyone who tried to help them, but they became docile and submissive to the vultures.

Those from this mob who had not been wounded and had tried to fight off the vultures began running from the scene of battle. This first encounter with the enemy was so devastating that I was tempted to join them in their flight. Then, incredibly fast, some of those who had fled began reappearing with full suits of armor on, holding large shields. This was the first bit of encouragement that I remember seeing.

These warriors who were returning no longer had the mirth of the party, but an awesome resolve had now replaced it. I knew that although these had been deceived once, they would not be easily deceived again. They began to take the places of those who had fallen and even began forming new ranks to protect the rear and flanks. This caused such great courage to spread through the army so that the determination of everyone to stand and fight again began to rise. Three great angels named Faith, Hope, and Love immediately came and stood behind the army. As we looked at them, all of our shields began to grow. It was amazing how quickly despair had turned to faith. It was a solid faith, too, tempered by experience.

The High Way

Now everyone had swords named "The Word of God" and arrows named for different biblical truths. We wanted to shoot back, but we did not know how to avoid hitting the Christians that the demons were riding on. Then it occurred to us that if these Christians were hit with Truth, they would wake up and fight off their oppressors. I fired off a few arrows, as did some of the others. Almost all the arrows hit Christians. However, when the arrows of Truth went into them, they did not wake up or fall down wounded—they became enraged and the demons riding on them grew much larger.

This shocked everyone, and we began to feel that this was an impossible battle to win. Even so, with Faith, Hope, and Love we were confident that we could at least hold our own ground. Another great angel named Wisdom appeared and directed us to fight from the mountain behind us.

On the mountain, there were ledges at different levels for as high as we could see. At each higher level the ledges became narrower and more difficult to stand on. Each level was named for a biblical truth. The lower levels were named after foundational truths such as Salvation, Sanctification, Prayer, and Faith, and the higher levels were named after deeper biblical truths. The higher we climbed, the larger both our shields and our swords grew, and fewer of the enemy arrows could reach our positions.

A Tragic Mistake

Some who had stayed on the lower levels began picking up the enemy arrows and shooting them back. This was a very grave mistake. The demons easily dodged the arrows and let them hit the Christians. When a Christian was hit by one of the arrows of accusation or slander, a demon of bitterness or rage would fly in and perch on that arrow. He would then begin to urinate and defecate his poison upon that Christian. When a Christian had two or three of these demons added to the pride or self-righteousness he already had, he was transformed into the contorted image of the demons themselves.

We could see this happening from the higher levels, but those on the lower levels who were using the enemy's arrows could not see it. About half of us decided to keep climbing, while the other half descended back to the lower levels to explain to those below what was happening. Everyone was then warned to keep climbing and not stop, except for a few who stationed themselves on each level to keep the other soldiers moving higher.

Safety at Last

When we reached the level called The Unity of the Brethren, none of the enemy's arrows could reach us. Many in our camp decided that this was as far as they needed to climb. I understood this because with each new level the footing was more precarious. However, I also felt much stronger and more skillful with my weapons as I went higher, so I continued climbing.

Soon my skills were good enough to shoot and hit the demons without hitting the Christians. I felt that if I kept going higher I could shoot far enough to hit the main leaders of the evil horde, who stayed behind their army. I regretted that so many had stopped on the lower levels where they were safe but could not hit the enemy. Meanwhile, the strength and character that grew in those who kept climbing made them great champions, each one able to destroy many of the enemy.

At each level there were arrows of Truth scattered about, which I knew were left from those who had fallen from that position (many had fallen from each position). All of the arrows were named after the Truth of that level.

Some were reluctant to pick up these arrows, but I knew we needed all we could get to destroy the great horde below.

I picked up one of the arrows, shot it, and easily hit a demon and the others also started picking up arrows and shooting them. We began to decimate several of the enemy divisions. Because of this, the entire evil army focused its attention on us. For a time it seemed that the more we achieved, the more the enemy attacked us. Though our task seemed endless, it had become exhilarating.

Since the enemy forces could not hit us with their arrows on the higher levels, swarms of vultures would fly above us to vomit down on us. Other vultures carried demons that would urinate or defecate upon the ledges, making them very slippery.

The Anchor

Our swords grew with each new level reached, but I almost left mine behind because I did not seem to need it at the higher levels. I casually decided to keep it, thinking that it must have been given to me for a reason. Then, because the ledge I was standing on was so narrow and slippery, I drove the sword into the ground and tied myself to it while I shot at the enemy.

The voice of the Lord then came to me, saying: *"You have used the wisdom that will enable you to keep climbing. Many have fallen because they did not use their swords properly to anchor themselves."* No one else seemed to hear this voice, but many saw what I had done and did the same.

I wondered why the Lord had not spoken to me to do this sooner. I then knew that He had already spoken this to me somehow. As I pondered this, I began to understand that my whole life had been training for this hour. I knew that I was prepared to the degree that I had listened to the Lord and obeyed His voice throughout my life. I also knew that for some reason the wisdom and understanding I now had could not be increased or taken away while in this battle. I was very thankful for every trial I had experienced in my life, and I was sorry for not appreciating them more at the time.

Soon we were hitting the demons with almost perfect accuracy. Rage ascended from the enemy army like fire and brimstone. I knew that the Christians trapped in that army were now feeling the brunt of that rage. Some of the demons became so angry that they were now shooting at each other. Normally this would have been very encouraging, but those who suffered the most were the deceived Christians in the camp of the enemy. I knew that to the world this was appearing to be an incomprehensible meltdown of Christianity itself.

Some of those who had not used their swords as anchors were able to strike down many of the vultures, but they were also more easily knocked from the ledges where they were standing. Some of these landed on a lower level, but some fell all the way to the bottom and were picked up and carried off by the vultures. I spent every free moment trying to drive my sword deeper into the ledge, or trying to tie myself more securely to it. Every time I did this, Wisdom would stand beside me, so I knew that it was very important.

A New Weapon

The arrows of Truth would seldom penetrate the vultures, but they hurt them enough to at least drive them back. Every time they were driven back far enough, some of us would climb to the next level. When we reached the level called Galatians Two Twenty, we were above the altitude that the vultures could withstand. At this level, the sky above almost blinded us with its brightness and beauty. I felt peace like I had never felt before.

Until I reached this level, my fighting spirit had been motivated almost as much by fear, hatred, or disgust for the enemy as it had been for the sake of the kingdom, truth, and love for the prisoners. But it was on this level I caught up to Faith, Hope, and Love, which before I had only been able to see from a distance. Here, I was almost overpowered by their glory. Even so, I felt that I could get close to them.

When I got next to Faith, Hope, and Love, they turned to me and began repairing and shining my armor. Soon it was transformed enough to brilliantly reflect the glory that was coming from them. When they touched my sword, great bolts of brilliant lightning began flashing from it.

Love then said, "Those who reach this level are entrusted with the powers of the age to come." Turning to me with a seriousness that was very sobering, he said, "I still must teach you how to use them."

The Galatians Two Twenty level was so wide that there did not seem to be any danger of falling. An unlimited supply of arrows was available, with the name Hope written on them. We shot some of them down at the vultures and killed them easily. About half of those who had reached this level kept shooting, while the others began carrying the arrows down to Christians still on the lower levels.

The vultures kept coming in waves upon the levels below, but with each wave there would be fewer than before. From Galatians Two Twenty we could hit any enemy in the army except the leaders themselves, who remained just out of our range. We decided not to use the arrows of Truth until we had destroyed all the vultures because the cloud of depression they created made the truth less effective. This took a very long time, but we did not get tired. Finally, it seemed as if the sky over the mountain was almost completely rid of the vultures.

Faith, Hope, and Love, who had grown like our weapons with each level, were now so large that I knew people far beyond the battle area could see them. Their glory even radiated into the camp of prisoners who were still under a great cloud of vultures. I was very encouraged that they could be seen this way. Maybe now the prisoners and the Christians who had been used by the enemy would understand that we were not the enemy, but they in fact had been used by him.

But this was not to be the case, at least not yet. Those in the camp of the enemy who began to see the light of Faith, Hope, and Love started calling them "angels of light" who were sent to deceive the weak or undiscerning. I knew then that their bondage was much greater than I had realized.

The non-Christians, who were not a part of either of these armies, saw the glory of Faith, Hope, and Love and started to come closer to the mountain to get a better view. Those who came closer to see them also started to understand what the battle had really been about. This was a great encouragement.

The Trap

The exhilaration of victory continued to grow in each of us. I felt that being in this army and in this battle had to be one of the greatest adventures of all time. After destroying most of the vultures that had been attacking our mountain, we began picking off the vultures that still covered the prisoners. As the cloud of darkness dissipated, the prisoners were bathed in sunlight and began to wake up as if they had been in a deep sleep. They were immediately repulsed by their condition, especially by the vomit that still covered them, and started cleaning themselves up. As they beheld Faith, Hope, and Love, they also saw the mountain and ran toward it.

Though the evil horde sent arrows of Accusation and Slander at their backs, the former prisoners did not stop. By the time they got to the mountain many had a dozen or more arrows stuck in them, yet they seemed to not even notice. As soon as they began to scale the mountain, their wounds began to heal. With the cloud of depression largely dispelled, it seemed as if everything was now getting much easier.

The former prisoners had great joy in their salvation. They seemed so overwhelmed with appreciation for each new level of the mountain that it gave us a greater appreciation for those truths too.

Soon a fierce resolve to fight the enemy arose in the former prisoners. They put on the armor provided and begged to be allowed to go back and attack the enemy who had held them captive and abused them for so long. We thought about it, but then decided we should all stay on the mountain to fight. Again, the voice of the Lord spoke, saying, *"A second time you have chosen wisdom. You cannot win if you try to fight the enemy on his own ground. You must remain on My holy mountain."*

I was stunned that we had made another decision of such importance just by thinking and briefly discussing it. I then resolved to do my best to not make another decision of any consequence without prayer. Wisdom then stepped up to me quickly, took both of my shoulders firmly, and looked me straight in the eyes, saying, *"You must do this!"*

As Wisdom said this to me, he pulled me forward as if he were saving me from something. I looked back and saw that, even though I had once been on the broad plateau of Galatians Two Twenty, I had drifted to the very edge without even knowing it. I had come very close to falling off the mountain. I looked again into the eyes of Wisdom, and he said with the utmost seriousness, *"Take heed when you think you stand, lest you fall. In this life you can fall from any level."*

I thought about Wisdom's words for quite a while. In the exuberance of the victory we were starting to achieve and the unity we were beginning to experience, I had become careless. It was more noble to fall because of the onslaught of the enemy than to fall because of carelessness.

The Serpents

For a long time, we continued killing the vultures and picking off the demons that were riding the Christians. We found that the arrows of different truths would have greater impact on different demons. We knew it was going to be a long battle, but we were not suffering any more casualties now, and we had continued to climb past the level of Patience.

It was troubling that after these Christians had the demons shot off of them, few would come to the mountain. Many had taken on the nature of the demons and continued in their delusion without them. As the darkness of the demons dissipated, we could see the ground moving around the feet of these Christians. Then I saw that their legs were bound by serpents. As I kept looking at the serpents, I saw that they were all the same kind and had the name Shame written on them.

We shot arrows of Truth at the serpents, but the arrows had little effect. We then tried the arrows of Hope, but without results. From Galatians Two Twenty it had been very easy to go higher because we all helped each other. Since there now seemed to be little that we could do against the enemy, we decided to just try to climb as far as we could until we found something that would work against the serpents.

We passed levels of truth very fast. On most of them we did not even bother to look around if there was not a weapon in sight that might work on the serpents. Faith, Hope, and Love stayed right with us, but I had not noticed that we had left Wisdom far behind. It would be a long time before I understood what a mistake this was. He would catch up to us on the top, but leaving him behind cost us a much quicker and easier victory over the evil horde.

The Beautiful Garden

Almost without warning, we came to a level that opened up into a Garden. It was the most beautiful place I had ever seen. Over the entrance to this Garden was written, "The Father's Unconditional Love." This entrance was so glorious and inviting that we could not resist entering. As soon as I entered, I saw a tree that I knew was the Tree of Life. It was in the middle of this Garden, and it was still guarded by angels of awesome power and authority. When I looked at them, they looked back. They seemed friendly, as if they had been expecting us. I looked back and there was now a host of other warriors in the Garden. This gave us all courage, and because of the angels' demeanor, we decided to pass them to get to the tree. One of the angels called out: "Those who make it to this level know the Father's love and can eat of the tree."

I did not realize how hungry I was. When I tasted the fruit, it was better than anything I had ever tasted. Yet it was also somehow familiar. It brought pleasant memories of such things as sunshine, rain, beautiful fields, and the sun setting over the ocean, but even more, it reminded me of the people I loved. With every bite, I loved everything and everyone more. Then my enemies started coming to mind, and I loved them too. The feeling was soon greater than anything I had ever experienced, even the peace we felt when we first reached the level of Galatians Two Twenty. Then I heard the voice of the Lord saying, *"This is now your daily bread. It will never be withheld from you. You may eat as much and as often as you like. There is no end to My love."*

I looked up into the tree to see where the voice had come from, and I saw that the tree was filled with pure white eagles. They had the most beautiful, penetrating eyes I have ever seen. They were looking at me as if waiting for instructions.

"They will do your bidding," one of the angels said. "These eagles eat snakes."

"Go!" I told the eagles. "Devour the shame that has bound our brothers."

They opened their wings, and a great wind came and lifted them into the air. The eagles filled the sky with a blinding glory. Even as high as we were, I could hear the sounds of terror from the enemy camp at the sight of the eagles descending.

The King Appears

The Lord Jesus Himself then appeared right in our midst. He took the time to greet each one personally, congratulating us for reaching the top of the mountain. Then He said to us, *"I must now share with you what I shared with your brothers after My resurrection—the message of My kingdom. The enemy's most powerful army has now been put to flight, but not destroyed. Now it is time for us to march forth with the gospel of My kingdom. The eagles have been released and will go with us. We will take arrows from every level, but remember that I am your Sword and your Captain. It is now time for the Sword of the Lord to be unsheathed."*

I then turned and saw that the entire army of the Lord was standing in the Garden. There were men, women, and children from all races and nations, each carrying their banners, which moved in the wind with perfect unity. I knew that nothing like this had been seen on the earth before. Although the enemy had many more armies and fortresses throughout the earth, I knew that none could stand before this great army of God.

Almost under my breath, I said, "This must be the day of the Lord." To my amazement, the whole host then answered in an awesome thunder: "The day of the Lord of hosts has come!"

Reflecting on the Dream

Months later, I sat pondering this dream. Alarmingly, certain events and conditions in the church had already seemed to parallel what I had seen when the hordes from hell began to march. I was then reminded of Abraham Lincoln. The only way he could become a great emancipator and the preserver of the Union was to be willing to fight a Civil War. Not only did he have to fight it, but he had to be determined not to compromise until the victory was complete.

Lincoln also had to have the grace to fight the bloodiest war in our history without "demonizing" the enemy with propaganda. If he had done that, he might have been able to galvanize the resolve of the North much faster, facilitating a quicker military victory. However, it would have made the reunion after the war much more difficult. Because he was truly fighting to preserve the Union, Lincoln never made the men and women of the South the enemy, but rather the evil that held them in bondage.

A great spiritual civil war now looms before the church. Many will do everything they can to avoid it. This is understandable and even noble. However, compromise will never maintain a lasting peace. It will only make the ultimate conflict that much more difficult when it comes, and it will come.

The Lord is now preparing courageous leaders who will be willing to fight a spiritual civil war in order to set men free. The main issue, as in the American Civil War, will be slavery versus freedom. The secondary issue, which will be the primary issue for some, will be money.

Just as the American Civil War at times looked like it would destroy the entire nation, that which is coming upon the church will sometimes appear as if it will bring the end of the church. However, just as the United States not only survived, but went on to become the most powerful nation on earth, the same is going to happen to the church. The church will not be destroyed, but the institutions and doctrines that have kept men in spiritual slavery will be.

Even after this, perfect justice in the church will not be attained overnight. There will still be struggles for women's rights and to set the church free from racism and exploitation. These are all causes that must be confronted. Yet in the midst of the coming spiritual civil war, Faith, Hope, and Love, and the kingdom of God they stand upon, will be seen as they never have before. This will begin drawing people to the kingdom. God's government is about to be demonstrated as greater than any human government.

Let us always remember that with the Lord "a thousand years is as a day" (see II Peter 3:8). He can do in us in one day what we think will take a thousand years. The work of liberating and raising up the church will be accomplished much quicker than we may think is humanly possible. However, we are not talking about human possibilities.

The Final Quest

Part II
THE HOLY
MOUNTAIN

We stood in the Garden of God under the Tree of Life. It seemed that the entire army was there, many of them kneeling before the Lord Jesus. He had just given us the charge to return to the battle for the sake of our brothers who were still bound and for the world that He loved. It was both a wonderful and a terrible command. It was wonderful because it came from Him. It was terrible because it meant that we would have to leave His manifest presence and the Garden that was more beautiful than any place we had ever been before. To leave all of this to go into battle again seemed incomprehensible.

The Lord continued His exhortation: *"I have given you spiritual gifts and power and an increasing understanding of My Word and My kingdom, but the greatest weapon you have been given is the Father's love. As long as you walk in My Father's love, you will never fail. The fruit of this tree is the Father's love, which is manifested in Me. This love, which is in Me, must be your daily bread."*

In this setting of such beauty and glory, it did not seem that the Lord was appearing in His glory. In fact, His appearance was rather ordinary. Even so, the grace with which He moved and spoke made Him the most attractive person I had ever seen. He was beyond human definition in dignity and nobility. It was easy to understand why He is everything that the Father loves and esteems. Seeing Him this way, so full of grace and truth, made it seem that nothing but grace and truth should ever matter.

As I ate the fruit from the Tree of Life, the thought of every good thing I had ever known filled my soul. When Jesus spoke, it was the same, only magnified. All I wanted to do was stay in this place and listen to Him. I remembered how I had once thought it must be boring for those angels who do nothing but worship Him continually before the throne. Now I knew that there was nothing more wonderful or exhilarating that we could ever do than to simply worship Him.

Such worship was what we were created for, and it would surely be the best part of heaven. I could not imagine how wonderful it would be if all of the heavenly choirs were added. It was hard to believe that I had struggled so much with boredom during worship services. I knew that it was only because I had been almost completely out of touch with this heavenly reality.

I was almost overwhelmed with the desire to go back and make up for those times during worship services when I had allowed my mind to wander or had occupied myself with other things. The desire to express my adoration for Him became almost insatiable. I had to praise Him! As I opened my mouth, I was shocked by the spontaneous worship that erupted from the entire army at the same time. I had almost forgotten that anyone else was there, yet we were all in perfect unity. The glorious worship that followed could not be described in human language.

As we worshiped, a golden glow began to emanate from the Lord. Then silver appeared around the gold. We were all then enveloped in colors, the richness of which I have never seen with my natural eyes. With this glory, I entered a realm of emotion that I had never experienced before. Somehow I understood that this glory had been there all along, but when we focused on Him in worship, we began to see more of His glory. The more intensely we worshiped, the more glory we beheld. If this was heaven, it was much, much better than I had ever dreamed.

His Dwelling Place

I have no idea how long this worship lasted. It could have been minutes or it could have been months. There was just no way to measure time in that kind of glory. I closed my eyes because the glory I was seeing with my heart was as great as what I was seeing with my physical eyes.

When I opened them, I was surprised to see that the Lord was not there any longer, but a troop of angels was standing where He had been. One of them approached me and said, "Close your eyes again." When I did, I beheld the glory of the Lord. This was no small relief. Now that I had experienced the glory, I knew I simply could not live without it.

Then the angel explained, "What you see with the eyes of your heart is more real than what you see with your physical eyes."

I had made this statement myself many times, but how little I had walked in it! The angel continued, "It was for this reason that the Lord told His first disciples it was better for Him to go away so that the Holy Spirit could come. The Lord dwells within you. You have taught this many times, but now you must live it for you have eaten from the Tree of Life."

The angel then began to lead me back to the gate. I protested that I did not want to leave. Seeming surprised, the angel took me by the shoulders and looked me in the eyes. This was when I recognized him—it was Wisdom.

"You never have to leave this Garden," he assured me. *"This Garden is in your heart because the Creator Himself is within you. You have desired the best part, to worship and to sit in His presence forever, and it will never be taken from you. But you must take it from here to where it is needed most."*

I knew he was right. I then looked past him to the Tree of Life. I had a compulsion to grab all of the fruit that I could before leaving. Knowing my thoughts, Wisdom gently shook me. *"No. Even this fruit, gathered in fear, would go bad. This fruit and this tree are within you because He is in you. You must believe."*

Seeing With Eyes Closed

I closed my eyes and tried to see the Lord again, but I could not. When I opened my eyes, Wisdom was still staring at me. With great patience, he continued.

"You have tasted of the heavenly realm, and no one ever wants to go back to the battle once they do. No one ever wants to leave the manifest presence of the Lord. After the Apostle Paul came here, he struggled for the rest of his life as to whether he should continue to labor for the sake of the church or return here to enter into his inheritance. His inheritance was magnified the longer he stayed and served on earth. Now that you have the heart of a true worshiper, you will always want to be here, and you can, whenever you enter into true worship. The more focused you are on Him, the more glory you will see, regardless of where you are."

Wisdom's words had finally calmed me. Again I closed my eyes just to thank the Lord for this wonderful experience and the life He had given to me. As I did, I started to see His glory again, and all of the emotion of the previous worship experience flooded my soul.

The Lord's words to me were so loud and clear that I was sure they were audible: *"I will never leave or forsake you."*

"Lord, forgive my unbelief," I responded. "Please help me never to leave or forsake *You*." This was both a wonderful and trying time. Here the "real world" was not real, and the spiritual realm was so much more real that I just could not imagine going back to the other. I was gripped both with wonder and a terrible fear that I might wake up at any moment and find it was all just a dream.

Wisdom understood what was going on inside of me. *"You are dreaming,"* he said. *"But this dream is more real than what you think of as real. The Father gave men dreams to help them see the door to His dwelling place. He will only dwell in men's hearts, and dreams can be a door to your heart, which will lead you to Him. This is why His angels so often appear to men in their dreams. In dreams they can bypass the fallen mind of man and go straight to his heart."*

As I opened my eyes, Wisdom was still gripping my shoulders. *"I am the primary gift that has been given to you for your work,"* he said. *"I will show you the way and keep you on it, but only love will keep you faithful. The fear of the Lord is the beginning of wisdom, but the highest wisdom is to love Him."*

Then Wisdom released me and started to walk toward the gate. I followed with ambivalence. I remembered the exhilaration of the battle and the climb up the mountain, and though it was compelling, there was no comparison to the presence of the Lord and the worship I had just experienced. Leaving this would be the greatest sacrifice I had ever made. Then I remembered how it was all inside of me, and I was amazed that I could forget this so quickly. It was as if a great battle was raging within me, between what I saw with my physical eyes and what I saw with my heart.

The Third Heaven

Having moved forward so that I was walking beside Wisdom, I asked him: "I have prayed for twenty-five years to be caught up into the third heaven like the Apostle Paul. Is this the third heaven?"

"This is part of it," he replied, *"but there is much more."*

"Will I be allowed to see more?" I asked.

"You will see much more. I am taking you to see more now," he replied.

I started thinking of the Book of Revelation. "Was John's revelation part of the third heaven?"

"Part of John's revelation was from the third heaven, but most of it was from the second heaven. The first heaven was before the fall of man. The second heaven is the spiritual realm during the reign of evil upon the earth. In the third heaven the love and domain of the Father will again prevail over the earth through the King."

"What was the first heaven like?" I inquired, strangely feeling a cold chill as I asked.

"It is wisdom not to be concerned about that now," Wisdom responded with increased seriousness, as my question seemed to jolt him. *"Wisdom is to seek to know the third heaven just as you have. There is much more to know about the third heaven than you can know in this life, yet it is the third*

heaven, the kingdom, that you must preach. In the ages to come you will be told about the first heaven, but it is not profitable for you to know about it now."

When I resolved to remember the cold chill I had just felt, Wisdom nodded, which I knew to be an affirmation of that thought. "What a great companion you are," I had to say as I realized the valuable gift that this angel was. "You really will keep me on the right path."

"I will indeed," he replied.

The Other Half of Love

I was sure I felt love coming from this angel, which was unique, since I had never felt it from the other angels. They usually showed their concern more out of duty than love. Wisdom responded to my thoughts as if I had spoken them out loud.

"It is wisdom to love, and I could not be Wisdom if I did not love you. It is also wisdom to behold the kindness and the severity of God. It is wisdom to love Him and to fear Him. You are in deception if you do otherwise. This is the next lesson that you must learn," he said with unmistakable earnestness.

"I do know that and have taught it many times," I responded, feeling for the first time that maybe Wisdom did not fully know me.

"I have been your companion for a very long time, and I know your teachings," Wisdom replied. *"Now you are about to learn what some of your own teachings mean. As you have*

said many times, 'It is not by believing in your mind, but in your heart that results in righteousness.'"

I apologized, feeling a bit ashamed at having questioned Wisdom. He graciously accepted my apology. It was then that I realized I had been questioning and challenging him most of my life, often to my harm.

"Just as there is a time to plant and a time to reap," Wisdom continued, *"there are times to adore the Lord, and there are times to honor Him with the greatest fear and respect. It is wisdom to know the time for each. True wisdom knows the times and seasons of God. I brought you here because it was time to worship the Lord in the glory of His love. This is what you needed the most after such a battle. I am now taking you to another place because it is time for you to worship Him in the fear of His judgment. Until you know both, there is a danger that we can be separated from each other."*

"Do you mean that if I had stayed back there in that glorious worship I would have lost you?" I asked in disbelief.

"Yes. I would have always visited with you when I could, but we would have rarely crossed paths. Although it is hard to leave such glory and peace, that is not the whole revelation of the King. He is both a Lion and a Lamb. To the spiritual children, He is the Lamb. To the maturing, He is the Lion. To the fully mature, He is both the Lion and the Lamb. Again, I know you understand this, but you have known it primarily in your mind. Soon you will know it in your heart, for you are about to experience the judgment seat of Christ."

Returning to the Battle

Before leaving the gates to the Garden, I asked Wisdom if I could sit for a while to ponder all that I had just experienced. *"Yes, you should do this,"* he replied, *"but I have a better place for you to do it."*

I followed Wisdom out of the gates and we began to go down the mountain. To my surprise, the battle was still going on, but not as intensely as it was when we ascended. There were still arrows of accusation and slander flying about on the lower levels, but most of the enemy horde that remained was furiously attacking the great white eagles. The eagles were easily prevailing.

We kept descending until we were almost at the bottom. Just above the levels of Salvation and Sanctification was the level of Thanksgiving and Praise. I remembered this level very well because one of the greatest attacks of the enemy came when I had first tried to reach it. Once we had arrived, the rest of the climb was much easier, and when an arrow penetrated our armor, healing came much faster.

As soon as my enemies spotted me on this level (they could not see Wisdom), a shower of arrows began to rain down on me. I knocked them down with my shield so easily that the enemies quit shooting. Their arrows were now almost gone, and they could not afford to waste them.

The soldiers who were still fighting from this level looked at me in astonishment with a deference that made me very uncomfortable. It was then I first noticed that the glory of the Lord was emanating from my armor and shield.

I told these soldiers to climb to the top of the mountain without stopping, and they also would see the Lord. As soon as they agreed to go, they saw Wisdom. They started to fall down to worship him, but he restrained them and sent them on their way.

The Faithful

I was filled with love for these soldiers, many of whom were women and children. Their armor was a mess, and they were covered in blood, but they had not given up. In fact, they were still cheerful and encouraged. I told them that they were deserving of more honor than I was because they had borne the greatest burden of the battle and had held their ground. They seemed to not believe me, but appreciated that I would say it. However, I really felt that it was true.

Every level on the mountain had to be occupied or the vultures that were left would come and desecrate it with vomit and excrement until it was difficult to stand on. Most of the ledges were occupied by soldiers which I recognized to be from different denominations or movements that emphasized the truth of the level they were defending. I was embarrassed by the attitude I had maintained toward some of these groups. I had considered them out of touch and backslidden at best, but here they were fighting faithfully against a terrible onslaught of the enemy. Their defense of these positions had probably enabled me to keep climbing.

Some of these levels were situated so that there was a good view of the mountain and the battlefield, but some were so isolated that the soldiers on them could see only their own position. These seemed unaware of the rest of the battle that was raging or the rest of the army that was also fighting the battle. They were so wounded from the slander and accusations that they would resist anyone who came down to them from a higher level to encourage them to continue climbing.

However, when some came down from the top, reflecting the glory of the Lord, the wounded warriors listened, most of them with great joy. Soon a number of them began to climb with courage and resolve. As I beheld all of this, Wisdom did not say much, but he seemed very interested in my reactions.

Reality Discovered

I watched as many soldiers who had been to the top began descending to all of the levels in order to relieve those who had been taking their stand on those truths. As they did, each level began to shine with the glory they carried. Soon the whole mountain was shining with a glory that was blinding to the vultures and demons that were left. After a time, there was so much glory on the mountain that it began to have the same feel as the Garden.

I started thanking and praising the Lord and immediately I was in His presence again. It was hard to contain the emotions and glory that I felt when I did this. The experience became so intense that I stopped. Wisdom was standing beside me. Putting his hand on my shoulder, he said, *"You enter His gates with thanksgiving and His courts with praise."*

"But that was so real!" I exclaimed. "I felt as if I was there again."

"You were there, indeed," replied Wisdom. *"It has not become more real, but you have. Just as the Lord told the thief on the cross, 'Today you will be with Me in Paradise,' you can enter Paradise at anytime. The Lord, His Paradise, and this mountain are all abiding in you, because He is in you. What were but foretastes are now a reality to you because you have climbed the mountain. The reason you can see me and others cannot, is not because I have entered your realm, but because you have entered mine. This is the reality that the prophets knew which gave them great boldness, even when they stood alone against armies. They saw the heavenly host that was for them, not just the earthly one arrayed against them."*

The Deadly Trap

I then looked out over the carnage below and the slowly retreating demonic army. Behind me, more of the glorious warriors were constantly taking their places on the mountain. I knew that we were now strong enough to attack and destroy what was left of this enemy horde. *"Not yet,"* said Wisdom. *"Look over there."*

I looked in the direction he was pointing but had to shield my eyes from the glory emanating from my own armor to see anything. Then I caught a glimpse of some movement in a small valley. I could not make out what I was seeing because the glory shining from my armor made it difficult to see into the darkness. I asked Wisdom if there was something that I could cover my armor with so I could see. He then gave me a very plain mantle to put on.

"What is this?" I inquired, a little insulted by its drabness.

"Humility," said Wisdom. *"You will not be able to see very well without it."*

Reluctantly I put it on and immediately I saw many things that I could not see before. I looked toward the valley and the movement I had seen. To my astonishment, there was an entire division of the enemy horde that was waiting to ambush anyone who ventured from the mountain.

"What army is that?" I asked, "and how did they escape the battle intact?"

"That is Pride," explained Wisdom. *"It is the hardest enemy to see after you have been in the glory. Those who refuse to put on this cloak will suffer much at the hands of that most devious enemy."*

As I looked back at the mountain, I saw many of the glorious warriors crossing the plain to attack the remnant of the enemy horde. None of them were wearing the cloaks of humility, and they had not seen the enemy that was ready to attack them from their rear. I started to run out to stop them, but Wisdom restrained me.

"You cannot stop this," he said. *"Only the soldiers who wear this cloak will recognize your authority. Come with me. There is something else that you must see before you can help lead in the great battle that is to come."*

The Foundation of Glory

Wisdom led me down the mountain to the very lowest level, which was named Salvation. *"You see this as the lowest level,"* declared Wisdom, *"but this is the foundation of the whole mountain. In any journey, the first step is the most important, and it is usually the most difficult. Without Salvation, there would be no mountain."*

I was appalled by the carnage on this level. Every soldier was very badly wounded, but none of them were dead. Multitudes were barely clinging to the edge. Many seemed ready to fall off, but none did. Angels were everywhere ministering to the soldiers with such great joy that I had to ask: "Why are they so happy?"

"These angels have beheld the courage that it took for these to hold on. They may not have gone any farther, but neither did they give up. They will soon be healed; then they will behold the glory of the rest of the mountain and they will begin to climb. These will be great warriors for the battle to come."

"But wouldn't they have been better off to climb the mountain with the rest of us?" I protested, seeing their present condition.

"It would have been better for them, but not for you. By staying here, they kept most of your enemies occupied and that made it easier for you to climb. Very few from the higher levels ever reached out to help others come to the mountain, but these did. Even when barely clinging to the mountain themselves, they would reach out to pull others up. In fact, most of the mighty warriors were led to the mountain by these faithful ones.

"These who stayed and faithfully fought on the level of Salvation are no less heroes than the ones who made it to the top. They brought great joy to heaven by leading others to salvation. It was for this reason that all the angels in heaven wanted to come to minister to them, but only the most honored were permitted."

Again I felt shame for my previous attitude toward these great saints. Many of us had scorned them as we climbed to the higher levels. They had made many mistakes during the battle, but they had also displayed more of the Shepherd's heart than the rest of us. The Lord would leave the ninety-nine to go after the one who was lost. These had stayed in the place where they could still reach the lost, and they paid a dear price for it. I also wanted to help but did not know where to start.

Wisdom then said, "It is right for you to want to help, but you will help most by going on to what you have been called to do. These will all be healed and will climb the mountain. They can now climb faster because of you and the others who went before them, both destroying the enemy and marking the way. They will join you again in the battle. These are fearless ones who will never retreat before the enemy."

The Power of Pride

I was pondering how I was learning as much by descending the mountain as I had by climbing it, when the noise from the battlefield drew my attention. By now, thousands of the mighty warriors had crossed the plain to attack the remnant of the enemy horde.

The enemy was fleeing in all directions, except for one division—Pride. Completely undetected, it had marched right up to the rear of the advancing warriors and was about to release a hail of arrows. I then noticed that the mighty warriors had no armor on their backsides. They were totally exposed and vulnerable to what was about to hit them.

Wisdom remarked, *"You have taught that there is no armor for the backside, which means you are vulnerable if you run from the enemy. However, you never saw how advancing in pride also makes you vulnerable."*

I could only nod in acknowledgment, for it was too late to do anything. It was almost unbearable to watch, but Wisdom said that I must. I knew the kingdom of God was about to suffer a major defeat. Though I had felt sorrow before, I had never felt this kind of sorrow.

To my amazement, when the arrows of Pride struck the warriors, they did not even notice. However, the enemy kept shooting. The warriors were bleeding and weakening fast, but they would not acknowledge it. Soon they were too weak to hold up their shields and swords; they cast them down, declaring that they no longer needed them. They started taking off their armor, saying it was not needed anymore either.

Then another enemy division appeared and moved up swiftly. It was called Strong Delusion. Its members released a hail of arrows and they all seemed to hit their marks. It only took a few of the demons of Delusion, who were all small and seemingly weak, to lead away this once great army of glorious warriors. They were taken to various prison camps, each named after a different doctrine of demons. I was astounded at how this great company of the righteous had been so easily defeated, and they still did not even know what had hit them.

I blurted out: "How could those who were so strong and have been all the way to the top of the mountain and have seen the Lord as they have, be so vulnerable?"

"Pride is the hardest enemy to see, and it always sneaks up behind you," Wisdom lamented. *"In some ways, those who have been to the greatest heights are in the greatest danger of falling. You must always remember that in this life you can fall at any time from any level."*

"Take heed when you think you stand, lest you fall," I replied. "How awesome such Scriptures seem to me now!"

"When you think you are the least vulnerable to falling is in fact when you are the most vulnerable. Most men fall immediately after a great victory," Wisdom lamented.

"How can we keep from being attacked like this?" I asked.

"Stay close to me, inquire of the Lord before making major decisions, and keep that mantle on. Then the enemy will not be able to easily blindside you as he did them."

I looked at my mantle. It looked so plain and insignificant. I felt that it made me look more like a homeless person than a warrior. Wisdom responded as if I had been speaking out loud.

"The Lord is closer to the homeless than to kings. You only have true strength to the degree that you walk in the grace of God, and 'He gives His grace to the humble.' No evil weapon can penetrate this mantle because nothing can overpower His grace. As long as you wear this mantle, you are safe from this kind of attack."

I then started to look up to see how many warriors were still on the mountain. I was shocked to see how few there were. I noticed, however, that they all had on the same mantle of humility. "How did that happen?" I inquired.

"When they saw the battle you just witnessed, they all came to me for help and I gave them their mantles," Wisdom replied.

"But I thought you were with me that whole time."

"I am with all who go forth to do the will of My Father," Wisdom answered.

"You're the Lord!" I cried.

"Yes," He answered. *"I told you that I would never leave you or forsake you. I am with all My warriors just as I am with you. I will be to you whatever you need to accomplish My will, and you have needed wisdom."* Then He vanished.

Rank in the Kingdom

I was left standing in the midst of the great company of angels who were ministering to the wounded on the level of Salvation. As I began to walk past these angels, they bowed on one knee and showed me great respect. I finally asked one of them why they did this, as even the smallest was much more powerful than I was. "Because of the mantle," he replied. "That is the highest rank in the kingdom."

"This is just a plain mantle," I protested.

"No!" the angel insisted. "You are clothed in the grace of God. There is no greater power than that!"

"But there are thousands of us all wearing the same mantle. How could it represent rank?" I asked.

"You are the dreaded champions, the sons and daughters of the King. He wore the same mantle when He walked on this earth. As long as you are clothed in that, there is no power in heaven or on earth that can stand before you. Everyone in heaven and hell recognizes that mantle. We are indeed His servants, but He abides in you, and you are clothed in His grace."

Somehow I knew that if I had not been wearing the mantle, and if my glorious armor had been exposed, the angel's statements and behavior toward me would have fed my pride. It was simply impossible to feel prideful or arrogant while wearing such a drab, plain cloak. However, my confidence in the mantle was growing fast.

The Holy Mountain

Part III

THE RETURN
OF THE EAGLES

On the horizon I saw a great white cloud approaching. Hope rose in me just from seeing it. Soon it had filled the whole atmosphere with hope, just as the rising sun chases away the darkness of night. As it grew closer, I recognized the great white eagles that had flown from the Tree of Life. They began landing on the mountain, taking their places on every level beside the companies of warriors.

I carefully approached the eagle that had landed near me because his presence was so awesome. When he looked at me with his penetrating eyes, I knew I could hide nothing from him. His eyes were so fierce and resolute that I trembled. Chills ran through me just from looking at him. Before I could even ask, he answered me.

"You want to know who we are. We are the hidden prophets who have been kept for this hour. We are the eyes of those who have been given the divinely powerful weapons. We have been shown all that the Lord is doing, and all that the enemy is planning against you. We have scoured the earth, and together we know all that needs to be known for the battle."

"Did you not see the battle that just took place?" I asked with as much irritation as I dared to express. "Couldn't you have helped those warriors who were just taken captive?"

"Yes," the eagle responded. "We saw it all, and we could have helped if they had wanted our help. We would have helped them by holding them back, telling them to sit and be still. But we can only fight in the battles that the Father commands, and we can only help those who believe in us. Only those who receive us as prophets can receive the prophets' reward or the benefit of our services. Those who were ambushed did not yet have the mantle you are wearing, and those who do not have that mantle cannot understand who we are. We all need one another, including these here who are still wounded, and many others whom you do not yet know."

The Eagle's Heart

As I talked to the eagle, I started to think like him. After this short discussion I could see into the eagle's heart and I began to know him like he knew me. The eagle recognized this.

"You have some of our gifts," the eagle noted, "though they are not very well developed. You have not used them much. I am here to awaken these gifts in you, and in many others like you, and I will teach you how to use them. In this way, our communication will be sure. Unless we have sure communication, we will all suffer many unnecessary losses, not to mention missing many great opportunities for victory."

"Where did you just come from?" I asked.

"We eat snakes," the eagle replied. "The enemy is bread for us. Our sustenance comes from doing the Father's will, which is to destroy the works of the devil. Every snake that we eat helps to increase our vision. Every stronghold of the enemy that we tear down strengthens us so we can soar higher and stay in the air longer. We have just come from a feast, devouring the serpents of Shame which have bound many of your brothers and sisters. They will be here soon. They are coming with the eagles we left behind to help them find the way and to protect them from the enemy's counterattacks."

These eagles were very sure of themselves, but not prideful. They knew who they were and what they were called to do. They also knew us and they knew the future. Their confidence was reassuring to me, but even more so to the wounded who were still lying all around us. Those who had recently been too weak to talk were actually sitting up and listening to my conversation with the eagle. They looked at him the same way lost children would look at their parents who had just found them.

The Wind of the Spirit

When the eagle looked upon the wounded, his countenance changed as well. In place of the fierce resoluteness he had previously exhibited, he became like a soft, compassionate, old grandfather. The eagle opened his wings and began to gently flap them, stirring up a cool, refreshing breeze that flowed over the wounded. It was unlike any other breeze I had ever felt before. With each breath I was gaining strength and clarity of mind. Soon the wounded were standing and worshiping God with a sincerity that brought tears to my eyes.

Again I felt a profound shame at having scorned those who stayed on this level. They had seemed so weak and foolish to those of us who were ascending the mountain, but they had endured much more than we had and remained faithful. God had kept them, and they loved Him with a great love.

I looked up at the mountain. The eagles were all gently flapping their wings. Everyone on the mountain was being refreshed by the breeze they were stirring up, and we all began to worship the Lord. At first there was some discord between the worship coming from the different levels, but soon everyone on every level was singing in perfect harmony.

Never on earth had I heard anything so beautiful. I never wanted it to end. Soon I recognized it as the same worship that we had known in the Garden, but now it sounded even richer and fuller. I knew this was because we were worshiping in the very presence of our enemies, in the midst of such darkness and evil surrounding the mountain.

I do not know how long this worship lasted, but eventually the eagles stopped flapping their wings and it ceased. "Why did you stop?" I asked the eagle I had been talking with.

"Because now they are whole," he replied, indicating the wounded who now were all standing and appeared to be in perfect condition. "True worship can heal any wound," he added.

"Please do it again," I begged.

"We will do this many times, but it is not for us to decide when. The breeze you felt was the Holy Spirit. He directs us; we do not direct Him. He has healed the wounded and has begun to bring about the unity that is required for the battles ahead. True worship also pours the precious oil upon the Head, Jesus. The oil then flows down over the entire body, making us one with Him and with each other.

"No one who comes into union with Him will remain wounded or unclean. His blood is pure life, and it flows through us when we are joined to Him. When we are joined to Him, we are also joined to the rest of the body so that His blood flows through us all. A wound is healed by closing the wound so blood can flow to the wounded member and bring regeneration. When a part of His body is wounded, we must join in unity with that part until it is fully restored. We are all one."

In the euphoria still left from the worship, this brief teaching seemed almost esoteric. Yet I knew it was very basic. When the Holy Spirit moved, every word seemed glorious, regardless of how elementary it was. I was so filled with love that I wanted to hug everyone, including the fierce old eagles.

Then, like a jolt, I remembered the mighty warriors who had just been captured. The eagle sensed this but did not say anything. He just watched me intently. Finally, I spoke up, "Can we recover those who were just lost?"

"Yes. It is right for you to feel what you do," the eagle finally said. "We are not complete and our worship is not complete until the whole body is restored. Even in the most glorious worship, even in the very presence of the King, we will all feel this emptiness until all are one because our King also feels it.

"We all grieve for our brothers in bondage, but we grieve even more for the heart of our King. Though you love each of your children, you would be particularly concerned for the one who was sick or wounded. The King loves all of His children too, but the wounded and oppressed have most of His attention now. For His sake, we must not quit until all have been recovered. As long as any are wounded, He is wounded."

Faith to Move the Mountain

Sitting down by the eagle, I pondered his words. Finally I remarked, "I know that Wisdom now speaks to me through you because I hear His voice when you speak. I was so sure of myself before that last battle, but I was almost carried away with the same presumption that they were carried away with. I could very easily have been captured with them if Wisdom had not stopped me.

"I was motivated more by hatred for the enemy than by the desire to set my brothers free. Since coming to this mountain and fighting in the great battle, I now think that most of the right things I did, I did for the wrong reasons, and many of the wrong things I did, I had good motives for. The more I learn, the more unsure of myself I feel."

"You must have been with Wisdom a long time," the eagle responded.

"He was with me a long time before I began to recognize Him, but I am afraid that most of that time I was resisting Him. Somehow I now know I am still lacking something very important, something I must have before I go into battle again, but I do not know what it is."

The great eagle's eyes became even more penetrating as he responded, "You also know the voice of Wisdom when He speaks to you in your own heart. You are learning well because you have the mantle. What you are feeling now is true faith."

"Faith?" I shot back. "I'm talking about serious doubts!"

"You are wise to doubt yourself. True faith depends on God, not on you and not even on your faith. You are close to the kind of faith that can move this mountain, and move it we must. It is time to carry it to places where it has not traveled before.

"However, you are right; you are still lacking something very important. You must yet have a revelation. Even though you have climbed to the top of the mountain and received from every truth along the way, and even though you have stood in the Garden of God and tasted of His unconditional love and seen His Son many times now, you still understand only a part of the whole counsel of God, and that only superficially."

I knew this was true, and it was actually comforting to hear it. "I have judged so many people and so many situations wrongly!" I exclaimed. "Wisdom has saved my life many times now, but the voice of Wisdom is still a very small voice within me, and the clamor of my own thoughts and feelings are still far too loud. I hear Wisdom speaking through you much louder than I hear Him in my own heart, so I know I must stay very close to you."

"We are here because you need us," the eagle replied. "We are also here because we need you. You have been given gifts I do not have, and I have been given gifts you do not have. You have experienced things I have not experienced, and I have experienced things that you have not. The eagles have been given to you until the end, and you have been given to us. I will be very close to you for a time and then you must receive other eagles in my place. Every eagle is different. It is together, not individually, that we have been given to know the secrets of the Lord."

The Doors of Truth

The eagle then rose up from the rock on which he had perched and soared over to the edge of the level on which we stood. "Come," he said. As I approached him, I saw steps that led down to the very base of the mountain, and a small door.

"Why have I not seen this before?" I asked.

"When you first came to the mountain you did not stay on this level long enough to look around," he answered.

"How did you know that? Were you here when I first came to the mountain?"

"I would have known if I had not been here, because all who miss this door do so for the same reason, but in fact, I was here," he responded. "I was one of the soldiers you so quickly passed on your way up the mountain."

It was then that I recognized the eagle as a man I had met and had a few conversations with soon after my conversion. He continued, "I wanted badly to follow you then, but I had been on this level for so long that I needed a change. I just could not leave all of the lost souls that I was still trying to lead here. When I finally committed myself to doing the Lord's will, whether it was to stay or go, Wisdom appeared to me and showed me this door. He said it was a shortcut to the top. That is how I was able to reach the top before you did. There I was changed into an eagle."

I then remembered that I had seen doors like this on a couple of the levels. I had even peeked into one of them and was amazed at what I saw. I did not venture very far into it because I was so focused on the battle and on trying to get to the top of the mountain. "Could I have entered one of those doors and gone right to the top?" I asked.

"It is not quite that easy," the eagle remarked, seeming a little irritated. "In every door there are passageways, one of which leads to the top." Anticipating my next question, he continued, "The other ones lead to the other levels on the mountain. The Father designed each passageway so that everyone would choose the one his level of maturity dictated."

"Incredible! How did He do that?" I thought to myself, but the eagle heard my thoughts.

"It was very simple," continued the eagle as if I had spoken my thoughts out loud. "Spiritual maturity is always determined by our willingness to sacrifice our own desires for the interests of the kingdom or for the sake of others. The door that requires the most sacrifice to enter will always take us to the highest level."

I was trying to remember all that the eagle was saying to me. I knew I must enter the door before me and that it would be wise to learn all I could from someone who had preceded me and had obviously chosen the correct door to the top.

"I did not go directly to the top, and I haven't met anyone who has," the eagle continued. "But I went there much faster than most because I had learned so much about self-sacrifice while fighting here on the level of Salvation. I have shown you this door because you wear the mantle and would have found it anyway, but time is short and I am here to help you mature quickly.

"There are doors on every level, and every one leads to treasures that are beyond your comprehension," he continued. "They cannot be acquired physically, but every treasure that you hold in your hands you will be able to carry in your heart. Your heart is meant to be the treasure house of God. By the time you reach the top again, your heart will contain treasures more valuable than all the treasures of the earth. They will never be taken from you; they are yours for eternity. Go quickly. The storm clouds are now gathering and another great battle is looming."

"Will you go with me?" I pleaded.

"No," he responded. "This is where I belong now. I must help these who were wounded. But I will see you here again. You will meet many of my brother and sister eagles before you return, and they will be able to help you better than I at the place where you meet them."

The Treasures of Heaven

I already loved the eagle so much that I could hardly stand to leave him. I was glad to know I would see him again. Now the door was drawing me like a magnet. I opened it and entered.

The glory I beheld was so stunning that I immediately fell to my knees. The gold, silver, and precious stones were far more beautiful than can be described. They actually rivaled the glory of the Tree of Life. The room was so large that it seemed to be without end. The floor was silver, the pillars were gold, and the ceiling was a single pure diamond that reflected every color I had ever known and many that I had not known. Angels without number were all around, dressed in various robes and uniforms that were of no earthly origin.

As I began to walk through the room, the angels all bowed in salute. One stepped forward and welcomed me by name. He explained that I could go anywhere in the room and see anything I wanted. Nothing was withheld from those who came through the door.

I was so overwhelmed by the beauty that I could not even speak. I finally remarked that this was even more beautiful than the Garden had been. Surprised, the angel responded, "This is the Garden! This is one of the rooms in your Father's house. We are your servants."

As I walked, a great company of angels followed me. I turned and asked the leader why they were following. "Because of the mantle," he said. "We have been given to you, to serve you here and in the battle to come."

I did not know what to do with the angels so I just continued walking. I was attracted to a large blue stone that appeared to have the sun and clouds inside of it. When I touched it, the same feelings flooded over me as when I had eaten the fruit of the Tree of Life. I felt energy, unearthly mental clarity, and love for everyone and everything. I started to behold the glory of the Lord. The longer I touched the stone, the more the glory increased. I never wanted to take my hand off the stone, but the glory became so intense that I finally had to draw away.

Then my eyes fell on a beautiful green stone. "What does that one have in it?" I asked the angel standing nearby.

"All of these stones are the treasures of salvation. You are now touching the heavenly realm, and that one is the restoration of life," he continued.

As I touched the green stone, I began to see the earth in rich and spectacular colors. They grew in richness the longer I had my hand on the stone, and my love for all that I saw also grew. Then I began to see a harmony among all living things on a level that I had never seen before. I began to see the glory of the Lord in the creation. It began to grow until again I had to step away because of the intensity.

Losing Track of Time

It occurred to me that I had no idea how long I had been there. I did know that my comprehension of God and His universe had grown substantially as I merely touched these two stones, and there were many, many more to touch. There was more in that one room than a person could have absorbed in a whole lifetime. "How many more rooms are there?" I asked the angel.

"There are rooms like this on every level of the mountain you climbed."

"How can one ever experience all that is in just one of these rooms, much less all of them?" I asked.

"You have forever to do this. The treasures contained in the most basic truths of the Lord Jesus are enough to last for more lifetimes than you can measure. No man can know all there is to know about any of them in just one lifetime, but you must take what you need and keep proceeding toward your destiny."

I started thinking about the impending battle again, and the warriors who had been captured. It was not a pleasant thought in such a glorious place, but I knew I would have forever to come back to this room. I had only a short time to find my way back to the top of the mountain and then back to the battlefront again.

I turned back to the angel and said, "You must help me find the door that leads to the top."

The angel looked perplexed. "We are your servants," he responded, "but you must lead us. This whole mountain is a mystery to us. We all desired to look into this great mystery, but after we leave this room we will be learning even more than you."

"Do you know where all the doors are?" I asked.

"Yes. But we do not know where they lead. There are some that look very inviting, some that are plain, and some that are actually repulsive. One is even terrible."

"In this glorious place there are doors that are repulsive?" I asked in disbelief. "And one that is terrible? How can that be?"

"We do not know, but I can show it to you," he responded.

"Please do," I said.

We walked for quite a while, passing treasures of unspeakable glory, all of which were difficult to bypass. There were also many doors with different biblical truths over each one. When the angel had called them "inviting,"

I felt that he had quite understated their appeal. I badly wanted to go through each one, but my curiosity about the "terrible door" kept me moving.

Then I saw it. "Terrible" had also been an understatement. Fear gripped me until I thought it would take my breath away.

Gethsemane

I turned away from that door and quickly retreated. There was a beautiful red stone nearby, which I almost lunged at to lay my hands on. Immediately, I was in the Garden of Gethsemane beholding the Lord in prayer. The agony I beheld was even more terrible than the door I had just seen. Shocked, I jerked my hand away from the stone and fell to the floor in exhaustion.

I wanted so badly to return to the blue or green stones, but I had to regain my energy and my sense of direction. The angels were quickly all around me, serving me. I was given a drink that began to revive me. Soon I was feeling well enough to stand and begin walking back to the other stones. However, the recurring vision of the Lord praying finally compelled me to stop.

"What was that back there?" I asked.

"When you touch the stones, we are able to see a little of what you see and feel a little of what you feel," said the angel. "We know that all these stones are great treasures, and the revelations they contain are priceless. We beheld for a moment the agony of the Lord before His crucifixion, and we briefly felt what He felt that terrible night. It is hard for us to understand how our God could ever suffer like that. It makes us appreciate much more what an honor it is to serve the men for whom He paid such a terrible price."

The angel's words were like lightning bolts straight to my soul. I had fought in the great battle. I had climbed to the top of the mountain. I had become so familiar with the spiritual realm that I hardly noticed angels anymore, and I could speak on nearly equal terms with the great eagles. Yet I could not bear to share even a moment of the sufferings of the Lord without wanting to flee to a more pleasurable experience. "I should not be here," I almost shouted. "I, more than anyone, deserve to be a prisoner of the evil one!"

"Sir," the angel said apprehensively, "we understand that no one is here because he deserves it. You are here because you were chosen before the foundation of the world for a purpose. We do not know what your specific purpose is, but we know that it is very great for everyone on this mountain."

"Thank you," I replied. "You are helpful. My emotions are being greatly stretched by this place, and they tend to overcome my understanding. You are right. No one is here because he is worthy. Truly, the higher we climb on this mountain, the more unworthy we are to be here and the more grace we need to stay. How did I ever make it to the top the first time?"

"Grace," my angel responded.

"If you want to help me," I said, "please keep repeating that word to me whenever you see me in confusion or despair. I am coming to understand that word better than any other.

"Now I must go back to the red stone," I continued. "I know now it is the greatest treasure in this room, and I must not leave until I am carrying that treasure in my heart."

The Truth of Grace

The time I spent at the red stone was the most painful ordeal I have ever experienced. Many times I simply could not take any more and had to withdraw my hand. Several times I went back to the blue or green stone to rejuvenate my soul before I returned. It was harder to return to the red stone each time, but my love for the Lord was growing more through this than anything I had ever learned or experienced.

Finally, when I saw the presence of the Father depart from Jesus on the cross, I could stand it no longer. I quit. I could tell that the angels, who were also experiencing what I was to a degree, were in full agreement with me. The willpower to touch the stone again simply was no longer in me. I did not even feel like going back to the blue stone. I just lay prostrate on the floor, weeping over what the Lord had gone through. I also wept because I knew that I had deserted Him just like His disciples. I failed Him when He needed me the most, just as they did.

After what seemed like several days, I opened my eyes. Another eagle was standing beside me. In front of him were three stones: one blue, one green, and one red.

"Eat them," the eagle said. When I did, my whole being was renewed, and great joy and great soberness flooded my soul.

When I stood up, I caught sight of the same three stones set into the handle of my sword and on each of my shoulders.

"These are now yours forever," the eagle said. "They cannot be taken from you, and you cannot lose them."

"But I did not finish this last one," I protested.

"Christ alone will ever finish that test," he replied. "You have done well enough, and you must go on now."

"Where to?" I asked.

"You must decide, but with the time getting shorter I suggest that you try to get to the top soon." The eagle then departed, obviously in a hurry.

I then remembered the doors. I started toward those that had been so appealing. But when I reached the first one, it did not appeal to me anymore. Then I went to another, and it felt the same. "Something seems to have changed," I remarked out loud.

"You have changed," the angels replied at once.

I turned to look at them and was amazed at how much they had changed. They no longer had a naive look about them, but were now more regal and wise-looking. I knew they reflected what had also taken place in me, but I now felt uncomfortable just thinking about myself.

"I ask for your counsel," I said to the leader.

"Listen to your heart," he said. "That is where these great truths now abide."

"I have never been able to trust my own heart," I responded. "It is subject to so many conflicts. I am too subject to delusion, deception, and selfish ambition. It is hard for me to even hear the Lord speaking to me above its clamor."

"Sir, with the red stone now in your heart, I do not believe that will continue to be the case," the leader offered with uncharacteristic confidence.

Judgment's Door

I leaned against the wall, thinking that the eagle was not here when I needed him the most. He had gone this way before and would know which door to choose. But I knew he would not come back, and I knew it was right that I choose. As I pondered my options, the "terrible door" was the only one I could think of. Out of curiosity I decided to go back and look at it. I had departed from it so fast the first time that I had not even noticed which truth it represented.

As I approached it, I could feel the fear welling up inside me, but not nearly as intensely as the first time. Unlike the other doors, it was very dark around this one, and I had to get very close to read the truth written over it. Mildly surprised, I read, "THE JUDGMENT SEAT OF CHRIST."

"Why is this truth so fearful?" I asked aloud, knowing that the angels would not answer me. As I continued looking at it, I knew that it was the one I should go through.

"There are many reasons it is fearful," the familiar voice of the eagle responded.

"I'm very glad you came back," I replied. "Have I made a poor choice?"

"No! You have chosen well," the eagle assured me. "This door will take you back to the top of the mountain faster than any other. It is fearful because the greatest fear in the creation has its source through that door. The greatest wisdom that men can know in this life, or in the life to come, is also found through that door. Even so, very few will go through it."

"But why is this door so dark?" I asked.

"The light of these doors reflects the attention that the church is presently giving to the truths behind them. The truth behind that door is one of the most neglected of these times, yet it is one of the most important. You will understand when you enter. The greatest authority that men can receive will be entrusted only to those who will go through this door. When you see Christ Jesus sitting on this throne, you will be prepared to sit with Him on it, too."

"Then this door would not be so dark and foreboding if we had just given more attention to this truth?" I asked.

"That is correct. If men knew the glory that is revealed behind that door, it would be one of the most brilliant," the eagle lamented. "However, it is still a difficult door to pass through. I was told to return and encourage you because soon you will need it. You will see a greater glory, but also a greater terror than you have ever known.

"Because you have chosen the difficult way now, it will be much easier for you later. Because you are willing to face this hard truth now, you will not suffer loss later. Many love to know His kindness, but very few are willing to know His severity. If you do not embrace *both*, you will always be in danger of deception and of a fall from His great grace."

"I know that I would never come here if I had not spent the time I did at the red stone. How could I keep trying to take the easy way when that is so contrary to the nature of the Lord?" I asked.

"But now you have chosen, so go quickly," the eagle told me. "Another great battle is about to begin, and you are needed at the front," he said.

As I looked at the eagle and saw the great resoluteness in his eyes, my confidence grew. Finally, I turned toward the door.

The Final Quest

Part IV

THE WHITE THRONE

Igazed one last time around the huge room inside the mountain. The gems and treasures that represented the truths of salvation were breathtaking in their glory. It seemed that there was no end to their expanse and no way to fully comprehend their beauty.

I could not imagine that the rooms which contained the other great truths of the faith could be any more glorious. This helped me to understand why so many Christians never wanted to leave this level, being content to just marvel at the basic doctrines of the faith. I knew that I could stay here for eternity and never get bored.

Then the eagle who was standing next to me exhorted, "You must go on!" As I turned to look at him, he lowered his voice and continued, "There is no greater peace and safety than to abide in the Lord's salvation. You were brought here to know this because you will need this faith for where you are now going. But you must not stay here any longer."

The eagle's statement about peace and safety caused me to think about the courageous warriors who had fought in the battle from the first level of the mountain, Salvation. Although they had fought so well and delivered so many, they had also all been badly wounded. It did not seem that they had found peace and safety here.

The eagle interrupted my thoughts again as if he were listening to them. "God has a different definition of peace and safety than we do," he said. "To be wounded in the fight is a great honor. It is by the Lord's stripes that we are healed, and it is through our stripes that we are also given the authority for healing. Once we are healed, we are given the power to heal others in the very place where the enemy wounded us.

"Healing was a basic part of the Lord's ministry, and it is also a basic part of ours. One reason why the Lord allows bad things to happen to His people is so they can receive compassion for others, by which the power of healing operates. That is why the Apostle Paul told of his beatings and stonings when his authority was questioned. Every wound and other bad things that happens to us can be turned into the authority to do good. Every beating that the great apostle took resulted in salvation for others. Every wound that a warrior receives will result in others being saved, healed, or restored."

The eagle's words were very encouraging. Standing here amid the glory of the treasures of salvation made this truth even clearer and more penetrating. I wanted to go shout it from the top of the mountain so that all who were still fighting would be encouraged.

Then the eagle continued, "There is another reason why the Lord allows us to be wounded. There is no courage unless there is real danger. The Lord said He would go with Joshua to fight for the Promised Land, but over and over He exhorted him to be strong and courageous. This was because he was going to have to fight, and there would be very real danger. It is in this way that the Lord proves those who are worthy of the promises."

The Glorious Eagle

I looked at the old eagle, and for the first time I noticed the scars among his torn and broken feathers. However, the scars were not ugly. They were lined with gold that was somehow not metal, but rather flesh and feathers. I could see that this gold was giving off the glory that emanated from the eagle and made his presence so awesome.

"Why did I not see this before?" I inquired.

"Until you have beheld and appreciated the depths of the treasures of salvation, you cannot see the glory that comes from suffering for the sake of the gospel. Once you have seen it, you are ready for the tests that will release the highest levels of spiritual authority into your life. These scars are the glory that we will carry forever. This is why even the wounds our Lord suffered are with Him in heaven. You can still see His wounds and the wounds that all of His chosen ones have taken for His sake.

"These are the medals of honor in heaven. All who carry them love God and His truth more than their own lives. These are the ones who followed the Lamb wherever He went, willing to suffer for the sake of truth, righteousness, and the salvation of men. True leaders of His people, who carry genuine spiritual authority, must have first proven their devotion this way."

I looked at the leader of the company of angels that followed me. I had never witnessed deep emotion in an angel before, but these words were unquestionably moving him greatly, as well as the rest of the angels. I really thought they were about to cry.

Then the leader spoke: "We have witnessed many wonders since the creation. But the voluntary suffering of men for the Lord and for their fellow men is the greatest wonder of all. We, too, must fight and even suffer at times, but we dwell where there is such light and glory that it is very easy to do this.

"When we see men and women choose to suffer for a hope that they can only dimly see in their hearts, it causes even the greatest angels to bow their knee and gladly serve these heirs of salvation. We marvel at the dedication of you who dwell with so little encouragement in a place of such darkness and evil.

"At first we did not understand why the Father decreed that men would have to walk by faith, suffering great opposition while not having the benefit of beholding the reality and the glories of the heavenly realm. But now we understand that through these sufferings He proves their worthiness to receive the great authority that they will be given as members of His own household.

"This walk of faith is now the greatest wonder in heaven. Those who pass this test are worthy to sit with the Lamb on His throne, for He has made them worthy and they have proven their love."

Courage

The eagle interjected, "Courage is a demonstration of faith. The Lord never promised that His way would be easy, but He has assured us that it would be worth it. The courage of those who fought from the level of Salvation moved the angels of heaven to esteem what God has brought about in fallen men. The faithful warriors took their wounds in the terrible onslaught, while only beholding darkness and a seeming defeat of the truth, just as our Lord did on His cross. Nevertheless, they did not quit, and they did not retreat."

I was again starting to regret that I had not remained on the level of Salvation and fought with those other brave souls. Once more, understanding my thoughts, the eagle interrupted them.

"By climbing the mountain, you were demonstrating faith and wisdom too. Your faith freed many souls so they could come to the mountain for salvation. You received some wounds, as the warriors on the level of Salvation did, but your authority in the kingdom has come more from acts of faith than from suffering. Because you have been faithful in a few things, now you will be given the great honor of going back to suffer, that you may be made a ruler over many more.

"But remember that we all work together for the same purposes, regardless of whether we are building or suffering. If you go higher, many more souls will fill these rooms to the great joy of heaven. You have now been called to climb and to build, but if you are faithful in this you will later be given the honor of suffering."

I then turned and looked at the dark and foreboding door over which was written, "THE JUDGMENT SEAT OF CHRIST." Just as warmth and peace had flooded my soul each time I looked at the great treasures of salvation, fear and insecurity gripped me when I looked at this door. Now it seemed that everything in me wanted to stay in this room, and nothing in me wanted to go through that door.

Again, the eagle answered my thoughts. "Before you enter the door to any great truth, you will have these same feelings. You even felt them when you entered into this room filled with the treasures of salvation. These fears are the result of the Fall. They are the fruit of the Tree of the Knowledge of Good and Evil. The knowledge from that tree made us all insecure and self-centered. The knowledge of good and evil makes the true knowledge of God seem fearsome, when in fact every truth from God leads to an even greater peace and security. Even the judgments of God are to be desired because all of His ways are perfect."

By now I had experienced enough to know that what seems right is usually the least fruitful path and is often the road to failure. Throughout my journey, the path of greatest risk was the path that led to the greatest reward. Even so, each time it seemed that more was at stake. Therefore, making the choice to go higher became more difficult each time. I started to sympathize with those who would stop at some point in their sojourn and refuse to go on, even though I knew more than ever that this was a mistake. The only true security came from continually moving forward into the realms that required more faith, which meant more dependence on the Lord.

"Yes, it takes more faith to walk in the higher realms of the Spirit," the eagle added. "The Lord gave us the map to His kingdom when He said, 'If you seek to save your life you will lose it, but if you will lose your life for My sake you will find it.' These words alone can keep you on the path to the top of the mountain and lead you to victory in the great battle ahead. They will also help you stand before the judgment seat of Christ."

Through the Door

I knew it was time for me to go. I resolved to always remember the glory of this chamber that contained the treasures of salvation, but I also knew that I had to move beyond them. I had to go on. I turned, and with all of the courage I could muster, opened the door to the judgment seat of Christ and stepped through it into terrifying darkness. The company of angels that had been assigned to me took positions all around the door, but did not enter.

"What's the matter? Aren't you coming?" I demanded.

"Where you are going now, you must go alone. We will be waiting for you on the other side."

Without responding, I turned and started walking before I could change my mind. Somehow I knew that I should not put my security in the company of angels. As I walked into the darkness, I heard the eagle's parting words, "After this you will not have your trust in anyone else, even yourself, but only in the Lord."

I immediately was in the most frightening darkness I had ever experienced. Each step became a terrible battle with fear. Soon I began to think I had stepped into hell itself. Finally I decided to retreat, but when I turned to go back, I could not see anything. The door was closed, and I could not even see where it was located. It was beginning to look as if everything that had happened to me, and everything the eagles and the angels had told me, had been a ruse to entrap me in this hell. I had been deceived!

I cried to the Lord to forgive me and help me. Immediately, I began to see Him on the cross, just as when I had laid my hand on the red stone in the chamber I had just left. Again I beheld the darkness of His soul as He stood alone, bearing the sin of the world. Although in the chamber this had been a terrible darkness to behold, now it was a light. I resolved to go on, fixing my mind on Him. As I did, peace began to grow in my heart with each step, and it became easier than it had been just a few minutes earlier.

Soon I was not even aware of the chilly darkness, and I started to see a dim light. Gradually it became a glorious light. Then it became so wonderful that I felt I was entering into heaven itself. The glory kept increasing as I walked along, and I wondered how anything this magnificent could have an entrance so dark and foreboding. Now I was enjoying every step.

The Great Hall

The path soon opened into a hall so large that I did not think the earth itself could contain it. Its beauty could not even be described by any reference to human architecture. This exceeded the wonder of anything I had yet experienced, including the Garden and the chamber that held the treasures of salvation.

By now I was as overwhelmed with joy and beauty as I had been overwhelmed by darkness and fear just minutes before. I then understood that every time I had experienced great pain or darkness of soul, it had been followed by a much greater revelation of glory and peace.

At the far end was the Source of the glory that was emanating from everything else in the room. I knew that it was the Lord Himself. Although I had now seen Him many times, I began to be a bit afraid as I walked toward Him. However, this fear was a holy fear that only magnified the great joy and peace that I also felt. Not only was the judgment seat of Christ a source of more security than I had ever experienced, but at the same time it was the source of a greater and purer fear.

I did not notice how great the distance was to the throne. It was so wonderful just to walk here that I did not care if it took me a thousand years to get there. In earthly terms, it did take me a very long time. In one sense, I felt that it was days, and in another, years. But somehow earthly time had no relevance here.

My eyes were so fixed on the glory of the Lord that I walked a long time before I noticed that I was passing multitudes of people who were standing in ranks to my left (there were just as many to my right, but they were so far away that I could not see them until I reached the throne). As I looked at them, I had to stop. They were dazzling, more regal than anyone I had ever seen. Their countenances were captivating.

Never had such peace and confidence graced human faces. Each one was beautiful beyond any earthly comparison. As I turned toward those who were close to me, they bowed in a greeting as though they recognized me.

"How is it that you know me?" I asked, surprised at my own boldness in asking them a question.

"You are one of the saints fighting in the last battle," a man close by responded. "Everyone here knows you, as well as all those who are now fighting on the earth. We are the saints who have served the Lord in the generations before you. We are the great cloud of witnesses who have been given the right to behold the last battle. We know all of you, and we see all that you do."

To my surprise, I recognized someone I had known on earth. He had been a faithful believer, but I did not think he had ever done anything of significance. He was so unattractive physically on earth that it made him shy. Here he had the same features, but was somehow more handsome than any person I had known on earth. He stepped up to me with an assurance and dignity that I had never seen before in him, or in any man.

"Heaven is much greater than we could have dreamed while on earth," he began. "This room is but the threshold of realms of glory that are far beyond our ability to comprehend. It is also true that the second death is much more terrible than we understood. Neither heaven nor hell are like we thought they were. If I had known on earth what I know here, I would not have lived the way I did. You are greatly blessed to be able to come here before you die," he said, looking at my garments.

I then looked at myself. I still had the old mantle of humility on, and the armor was still under it. I felt both foul and crude standing before those who were so glorious. I began to think that I was in serious trouble if I was going to appear before the Lord like this. Like the eagles, my old acquaintance could understand my thoughts, and he responded to them.

"Those who come here wearing that mantle have nothing to fear. That mantle is the highest rank of honor, and it is why they all bowed to you when you passed."

"I did not notice anyone bowing to me," I replied, a bit disconcerted. "In fact, I didn't even notice anyone until just now."

"It is not improper for someone to bow down before you," he continued. "Here we show each other the respect that is due. Even the angels serve us here, but only our God and His Christ are worshiped. There is a marked difference between honoring others in love, and worshiping them. If we had understood this on earth, we would have treated others very differently. It is here in the light of His glory that we can fully perceive and understand each other so we can relate properly."

Foolish Virgins

I was still ashamed. I had to restrain myself to keep from bowing down to those in the great hall, while at the same time wanting to hide myself because I felt so lowly. Then I began lamenting the fact that my thoughts were just as foolish here as they were on the earth, and here everyone knew them! I felt both stained and stupid standing before these who were so awesome and pure. Again my old acquaintance responded to these thoughts.

"We have our incorruptible bodies now, and you do not. Our minds are no longer hindered by sin. We are therefore able to easily comprehend what even the greatest earthly mind cannot fathom, and we will spend eternity growing in our ability to understand. This is so we can know the Father and understand the glory of His creation. On earth you cannot even begin to understand what the least of these know here. In fact, we are the least of those here."

"How could you be the least?" I asked with disbelief.

"There is an aristocracy of sorts here," he answered. "The rewards for our earthly lives are the eternal positions that we will have forever. This great multitude are those whom the

Lord called 'foolish virgins.' We knew the Lord and trusted in His cross for salvation, but we lived for ourselves more than we really lived for Him. We did not keep our vessels filled with the oil of the Holy Spirit. We have eternal life, but we wasted our lives on earth."

I was greatly surprised by what he was telling me, but I knew that no one could lie in this place.

"The foolish virgins gnashed their teeth in the *outer darkness*," I protested.

"And that we did. The grief that we experienced when we understood how we had so wasted our lives was beyond any grief possible on earth. The darkness of that grief can only be understood by those who have experienced it. Such darkness is magnified when it is revealed next to the glory of the One we failed.

"You are standing among those in the lowest rank of heaven. There is no greater folly than to know the great salvation of God, but to then go on living for yourself. To come here and learn the reality of that is grief beyond what an earthly soul can experience. We are those who suffered outer darkness because of this greatest of follies."

I was still incredulous. "But you are more glorious and full of joy and peace than I ever imagined, even for those in heaven. I do not sense any remorse in you, and yet I know that here you cannot lie. This does not make sense to me."

Looking me straight in the eyes, he continued, "The Lord also loves us with a love greater than you can yet understand. Before His judgment seat I tasted the greatest remorse and darkness of soul that can be experienced. Though here we do not measure time as you do, it seemed to last for as long as my life on earth had lasted. All my sins and follies that I had not repented of passed before me and before all who are here.

"You cannot understand the grief of this until you have experienced it," he went on. "I felt that I was in the deepest dungeon of hell, even as I stood before the glory of the Lord. He was resolute until my life had been completely reviewed. When I said I was sorry and asked for the mercy of His cross, He wiped away my tears and took away the darkness. I no longer feel the bitterness that I knew as I stood before Him, but I remember it.

"Here you can remember such things without continuing to feel the pain. A moment in the lowest part of heaven is much greater than a thousand years of the highest life on earth. Now my mourning at my folly has been turned into joy, and I know that I will experience joy forever, even if I am in the lowest place in heaven."

I began to think again of the treasures of salvation. Somehow I knew that all this man had told me was revealed by those treasures. Every step I had taken up the mountain, or into it, had revealed that His ways are both more fearful and more wonderful than I had ever been able to comprehend before.

Looking at me intently, my former acquaintance continued: "You are not here just to gain understanding, but to be changed. The next level of rank has glory many times greater than what we have here. Each new level is that much greater than the previous one. It is not just that those on each level have a more glorious spiritual body, but that each level is closer to the throne from where all the glory comes.

"Even so, I no longer feel the grief of my failure. I really deserve nothing. I am here by grace alone, and I am so thankful for what I have. He is so worthy to be loved. I could be doing many wondrous things now in the different realms of heaven, but I would rather stay here and just behold His glory, even if I am on the outer fringes."

Then, with a distant look in his eyes, he added, "Everyone in heaven is now in this room to watch His great mystery unfold, and to watch those of you who will fight the last battle."

"Can you see Him from here?" I asked. "I see His glory far away, but I cannot see Him."

"I can see many times better than you can," he answered. "And yes, I can see Him and hear Him. I can see all that He is doing. He also gave us power to observe what is happening on earth. We are the great cloud of witnesses who are watching you and cheering you on."

He bowed and then returned to the ranks. I began walking again, trying to understand all that he had said to me. As I looked over the great host that he said were the foolish virgins, the ones who had spiritually slept away their lives on earth, I knew that if any one of them appeared on earth now they would be worshiped as gods. Yet they were the very least of those who were here!

I then began to think of all of the time that I had wasted in my own life. It was such an overwhelming thought that I stopped. Then parts of my life began to pass before me. I began to experience a terrible grief over my sin. I, too, had been one of the greatest of fools! I may have kept more oil in my lamp than others, but now I knew how foolish I had been to measure what was required of me by how others were doing. I was one of the foolish virgins also!

The Would-Be Mentor

Just when I thought I would collapse under the weight of this terrible discovery, a man I had known and esteemed as a great man of God came forward to steady me. As he greeted me warmly, his touch somehow revived me.

I had wanted to be discipled by this man, but we did not get along well. As had happened with a number of other men of God that I tried to get close to, I was an irritation to this man, and he had finally asked me to leave. For years I had felt guilty about this, convinced that I had missed a great opportunity because of some flaw in my character. Even though I had put it out of my mind, I still carried the weight of this failure. When I saw him, it all surfaced and a sick feeling came over me. Now he was so regal that I felt even more repulsive and embarrassed by my poor condition. I wanted to hide, but there was no way I could avoid him here.

To my surprise, his warmth toward me was so genuine that he soon put me at ease. There did not seem to be any barriers between us. In fact, the love I felt coming from him almost completely took away my self-consciousness.

"I have waited eagerly for this meeting," he said.

"You were waiting for me?" I asked. "Why?"

"You are just one of many that I am waiting for. I did not understand until my judgment that you were one that I was called to help—to even disciple, but I rejected you."

"Sir," I protested, "it would have been a great honor to have been discipled by you, and I am very thankful for the time I did have with you. But I was so arrogant that I deserved the rejection. I know my rebellion and pride have prevented me from having a real spiritual father. This was not your fault, but mine."

"It is true you were prideful, but that is not why I was offended with you," he said. "I was offended because of my insecurity, which made me want to control everyone around me. I was offended that you would not accept everything I said without questioning it. I then started to look for anything that was wrong with you so I could justify rejecting you. I began to feel that if I could not control you, one day you would embarrass me and my ministry. I esteemed my ministry more than I did the people for whom it was given to me, so I drove you and many others like you away."

"I must admit that at times I thought you had turned into a…" I stopped myself, embarrassed by what I was about to say.

"And you were right," he said with a genuineness that is unknown in the realms of earth. "I had been given the grace to be a spiritual father, but I was a very poor one. All children are rebellious. They are all self-centered and think the world revolves around them. That is why they need parents to raise them. Almost every child will, at times, bring reproach on his family, but he is still a part of the family.

"I turned away many of God's own children—precious people He had entrusted to me so they could be brought to maturity. I failed with many of those who stayed with me. Most of them suffered terrible and unnecessary wounds and failures that I could have helped them avoid. Many of them are now prisoners of the enemy.

"I built a large organization," he continued, "and had considerable influence in the church. But the greatest gifts the Lord entrusted to me were the people who were sent to me for discipling, many of whom I rejected.

"Had I not been so self-centered and concerned with my own reputation, I would be a king here. I was called to sit on one of the highest thrones. All that you have and will accomplish would have been in my heavenly account as well. Instead, much of what I gave my attention to was of very little eternal significance."

"What you accomplished was astounding," I interjected.

"What looks good on earth looks very different here. What will make you a king on earth will often be a stumbling block to keep you from being a king here. What will make you a king here is lowly and unacclaimed on earth. I failed some of the greatest tests and greatest opportunities that were given to me, one of which was you. Will you forgive me?"

"Of course," I said, embarrassed. "But I am in need of your forgiveness too. I still think it was my awkwardness and rebellion that made it difficult for you. In fact, I, too, have failed to let some people get close to me who wanted to for the same reasons you did not want me around you."

"It is true that you were not perfect," he replied, "and I discerned some of your problems rightly, but that is never reason to reject someone. The Lord did not reject the world when He saw its failures. He did not reject me when He saw my sin. He laid down His life for me. It is always the greater who must lay down his life for the lesser. Even though I was more mature and had more authority than you, I became like one of the goats in the parable, rejecting the Lord by rejecting you and many others He sent to me."

As he talked, his words were striking me deeply. I, too, was guilty of everything he mentioned. Passing through my mind were the faces of many young men and women I had brushed off as not being important enough for my time. I desperately wanted to return and gather them together!

The grief I began to feel was even worse than how I had felt about wasting my time. I had wasted people! Now many of these were prisoners of the enemy, wounded and captured during the battle on the mountain. This whole battle was for the people, and yet people are often our least concern. We will fight for truths more than for the people for whom the truths are given. We will fight for ministries, while running roughshod over the people in them.

"And many people think of me as a spiritual leader! I am truly the least of the saints," I thought out loud.

The Enemy of the Gospel

"I understand how you feel," remarked another man. I recognized him as someone I had considered as one of the greatest Christian leaders of all time. "Paul the Apostle said near the end of his life that he was the least of the saints. Then, just before his death, he even called himself 'the greatest of sinners.' If he had not learned that lesson during his life on earth, he, too, would have been in jeopardy of becoming one of the least of the saints in heaven. Because he learned it on earth, he is now one of those closest to the Lord and will be one of the highest in rank for all of eternity."

Seeing this man in the company of the foolish virgins was the greatest surprise yet. "I cannot believe that you, too, are one of the foolish who slept away their lives on earth. Why are you here?"

"I am here because I made one of the gravest mistakes you can make as one entrusted with the glorious gospel of our Savior," he answered. "Just as the Apostle Paul progressed from not considering himself inferior to the greatest apostles, to being the greatest of sinners, I took the opposite course. I started out knowing that I had been one of the greatest of sinners who had found grace, but ended up thinking that I was one of the greatest apostles. It was because of my great pride, not insecurity like our friend here, that I began to attack everyone who did not see everything just the way I did.

"I stripped those who followed me of their own callings and even their personalities, pressuring them all to become just like me. No one around me could be himself. No one dared to question me because they knew I would crush them into powder. I thought by making others smaller I made myself greater. I thought that I was supposed to be the Holy Spirit to everyone.

"From the outside my ministry looked like a smooth running machine where everyone was in unity and there was perfect order, but it was the order of a concentration camp. I took the Lord's children and made them automatons. I molded them into my own image instead of His. In the end I was not even serving the Lord, but rather the idol I had built to myself. By the end of my life I was actually an enemy of the true gospel, at least in practice, even if my teachings and writings seemed impeccably biblical."

Coming from this person, such statements astounded me. I began to wonder if every meeting I had here was meant to give me a greater shock than the previous one.

"If it is true that you became an enemy of the gospel, how is it that you are still here?" I questioned.

"By the grace of God, I did trust in the cross for my own salvation. However, I actually kept other men from it, leading them to myself rather than to the Lord. Even so, the blessed Savior remains faithful to us even when we are unfaithful. It was also by His grace that the Lord took me from the earth sooner than He would have, just so those who were under me could find Him and come to know Him."

Through a Glass Darkly

I could not have been more stunned to think that this particular man was guilty of such things. History had given us a very different picture of him.

Reading what was going on in my heart, he continued: "God does have a different set of history books than those on the earth. You have had a glimpse of this, but you do not yet know how different they are. Earthly histories will pass away, but the books that are kept here will last forever. If you can rejoice in what heaven is recording about your life, you are blessed indeed. Men see through a glass darkly, so their histories will always be clouded and sometimes completely wrong."

"How was it that so many other leaders esteemed you so?" I inquired, still having trouble absorbing what I was hearing.

"Very few Christians, even very few leaders, have the true gift of discernment. Without this gift it is impossible to accurately discern truth in those of the present or the past. Even with this gift it is difficult. Until we have been here and been stripped, we will judge others through distorted prejudices, either positive or negative. That is why we were warned not to judge before the time.

"Until we have been here, we cannot really know what is in the hearts of others and whether they are performing good or evil deeds. There have been good motives in even the worst of men and evil motives in even the best of them. Only here can men be judged by both their deeds and their motives."

"When I return to earth, will I be able to discern history accurately because I have been here?"

"You are here because you prayed for the Lord to judge you severely, to correct you ruthlessly, so that you could serve Him more perfectly. This was one of the wisest requests you have ever made. The wise judge themselves lest they be judged. The even wiser ask for the judgments of the Lord because they realize they cannot even judge themselves well.

"Having come here, you will leave with far more wisdom and discernment, but on earth you will always see through a glass darkly, at least to some degree. Although your experience here will help you to know men better, only when you are fully here can you know them fully. When you leave here you will be more impressed by how little you know men rather than by how well you know them. This is just as true in relation to the histories of men. I have been allowed to talk with you because I have, in a sense, discipled you through my writings, and knowing the truth about me will help you," the famous Reformer concluded.

The Reformer's Wife

Then a woman I did not know stepped forward. Her beauty and grace were breathtaking but not in a sensual or seductive way.

"I was his wife on earth," she began. "Much of what you know of him actually came from me. Therefore, what I am about to say is not just about him, but about us. You can reform the church without reforming your own soul. You can dictate the course of history and yet not do the Father's will or glorify His Son. If you commit yourself to making human history, you may do it, but it is a fleeting accomplishment that will evaporate like a wisp of smoke."

"But your husband's work, or your work, greatly impacted every generation after him for good. It is hard to imagine how dark the world would have been without him," I protested.

"True," she answered. "But you can gain the whole world and still lose your own soul. Only if you keep your own soul pure can you truly impact the world for the eternal purposes of God. My husband lost his soul to me, and he only regained it at the end of his life because I was taken from the earth so that he could.

"Much of what my husband did, he did more for me than for the Lord. I pressured him and even gave him much of the knowledge that he taught. I used him as an extension of my own ego because as a woman I could not be recognized at the time as a spiritual leader myself. In a sense, I took over his life so that I could live my life through him. Soon I had him doing everything just to prove himself to me."

"You must have loved her very much," I said, looking at him.

"No, I did not love her at all," he said to my amazement. "Neither did she love me. In fact, after just a few years of marriage we did not even like each other. But we both needed each other, so we found a way to work together. Our marriage was not a yoke of love, but of bondage. The more successful we became, the more unhappy we became, and the more deception we used to fool those who followed us. We were empty wretches by the end of our lives.

"The more influence you gain by your own self-promotion, the more you must strive to retain your influence, and the more your life will become dark and cruel. Kings feared us, but we feared everyone, from the kings to the peasants. We could trust no one because we were living in such deception ourselves that we did not even trust each other. We preached love and trust because we wanted everyone to love and trust us. But we, ourselves, secretly feared and despised everyone. If you preach the greatest truths but do not live them, you are only the greatest hypocrite and the most tormented soul."

Their words pounded me like a hammer. I could see that my life was already heading in the same direction. How much was I doing to promote myself rather than Christ? I began to see how much I did just to prove myself to others, especially those I felt in competition with or those who disliked or rejected me. I began to see how much of my own life was built on the facade of a projected image that belied who I really was. But here I could not hide. This great cloud of witnesses all knew who I was beyond the veil of my projected motives.

I looked again at this couple. They were now so guileless and so noble that it was impossible to question their motives. They gladly exposed their most devious sins for my sake and were genuinely happy to be able to do it.

"I may have had a wrong concept of you from your history and your writings, but I have even more esteem for you now," I told them. "I pray that I can carry from this place the integrity and freedom that you now have. I am tired of trying to live up to projected images of myself. How I long for that freedom!" I lamented, wanting desperately to remember every detail of this encounter.

The High Calling

Then the famous Reformer offered a final exhortation: "Do not try to teach others to do what you, yourself, are not doing. Reformation is not just a doctrine. True reformation only comes from union with the Savior. When you are yoked with Christ, carrying the burdens that He gives you, He will be with you and carry them for you. You can only do His work when you are doing it *with* Him, not just *for* Him.

"Only the Spirit can beget that which is Spirit. If you are truly yoked with Him, you will do nothing for the sake of politics or history. Anything you do because of political pressures or opportunities will only lead you to the end of your true ministry. The things that are done in an effort to make history will at best confine your accomplishments to history, and you will fail to impact eternity. If you do not live what you preach to others, you disqualify yourself from the high calling of God, just as we did."

"I do not think I could even consider seeking a high calling," I interrupted. "I don't even deserve to sit here in this place that you say is for the *lowest* rank in heaven. How could I ever consider seeking a high calling?"

"The high calling is not out of reach for anyone that the Lord has called. I will tell you what will keep you on the path of life—love the Savior and seek His glory alone. Everything you do to exalt yourself will one day bring you the most terrible humiliation. Everything you do out of genuine love for the Savior, to glorify His name, will extend the limits of His eternal kingdom and ultimately result in a much higher place for yourself. Live for what is recorded here. Care nothing for what is recorded on earth."

The couple then parted with a cheerful embrace, yet I felt anything but cheerful. As they walked away, I was again overwhelmed by my own sin. Memories of the times I had used people for my own purposes, or even used the name of Jesus to further my own ambitions, or make myself look better, began to cascade down upon me. Here, in this place where I could behold the power and glory of the One I had so used, such memories became more repulsive than I could stand. I fell on my face in the worst despair I had ever known.

After what seemed like an eternity of seeing people and events pass before me, I felt the Reformer's wife lifting me to my feet again. I was overcome by her purity, especially as I now felt so evil and corrupt. I had the strongest desire to worship her because she was so pure.

"Turn to the Son," she said emphatically. "Your desire to worship me, or anyone else at this time, is only an attempt to turn the attention away from yourself and justify yourself by serving what you are not. I am pure now because I turned to Him. You need to see the corruption that is in your own soul, but then you must not dwell on yourself or seek to justify yourself with dead works, but turn to Him."

She said this with such genuine love that it was impossible to be hurt or offended by it. When she saw that I understood, she continued.

"The purity you see in me was what my husband first saw in me when we were young. I was relatively pure in my motives then, but I corrupted his love and my own purity by allowing him to worship me wrongly. You can never become pure by worshiping those who are more pure than yourself. You must go beyond them to find the One who has *made them* pure, and in whom alone there is no sin.

"The more people praised us, and the more we accepted their praises, the further we drifted from the path of life. Then we started living for the praises of men and to gain power over those who would not praise us. That was our demise, and it is the same for many who are here in the lowest place."

Purified Love

Simply wanting to prolong our conversation, I asked the next question that came to my mind: "Is it difficult for you and your husband to be here together?"

"Not at all," she responded. "All the relationships you have on earth are continued here. They are all purified by the judgment and by the fact that they are now spiritual, just as we are now spirit. The more you are forgiven, the more you love. After we forgave each other, we loved each other more. Now our relationship is continuing in much greater depth and richness because we are joint heirs of this salvation.

"As deep as the wounds were that we afflicted upon each other, that was how deep the love was able to reach when we were healed. We could have experienced this on earth, but we did not learn forgiveness in time. If we had learned forgiveness, the competition that entered our relationship and sidetracked our lives would not have been able to take root in us. If you truly love, you will truly forgive. The harder it is for you to forgive, the further you are from true love. Forgiveness is essential, or you will stumble and stray from the course chosen for you."

I realized that this woman, who had brought me into such confrontation with the pain of my own depravity, was also the most attractive person I could ever remember meeting. It was not romantic attraction, but I just did not want to leave her. Perceiving my thoughts, she withdrew a step, indicating that she was about to go. Before leaving, she offered me some final insights.

"The pure truth, spoken in pure love, will always attract," she said. "You will remember the pain you feel here, and it will help you through the rest of your life. Pain is good; it shows you where there is a problem. Do not try to reduce the pain until you find the problem. God's truth often brings pain as it highlights a problem that we have, but His truth will always show us the way to freedom too. When you know this, you will even begin to rejoice in your trials, which are all allowed to help keep you on the path of life.

"Your attraction to me is not out of order. It is the attraction between male and female that was given in the beginning, which is pure in its original form. When pure truth is combined with pure love, men can be the men they were created to be without having to dominate women out of insecurity. Such domination is nothing but lust, which is the lowest depth to which love falls because of our sin. With true love, men become true men. Women, likewise, can be the women they were created to be because their love has replaced their fear.

"Love will never manipulate or try to control out of insecurity because love casts out all fear. The very place where relationships can be the most corrupted is also where they can be the most fulfilling, after redemption has worked in them. True love is a taste of heaven, and lust is the enemy's ultimate perversion of the glory of heaven. To the degree that you are free of lust on earth, you will begin to experience heaven."

"But I do not think I have felt any lust for you or for *anyone* while I've been here," I mildly protested. "On the contrary, I was marveling that I could behold one with your beauty and not feel lust."

"That is because you are here. The light of His glory here casts out all darkness, but if you were not here, lust would be gripping you now," she said.

"I'm sure you are right. Can we ever be free from this terrible perversion on earth?" I begged.

"Yes. As your mind is renewed by the Spirit of Truth, you will not see relationships as opportunities to *take* from others, but to give. Giving provides the greatest fulfillment that we can ever know. The most wonderful human relationships are but fleeting glimpses of the ecstasy that comes when we give ourselves to the Lord in pure worship. What we experience in worship here, your frail, unglorified body could not endure. The true worship of God will purify the soul for the glory of true relationships.

"Therefore, you must not seek relationships, but true worship. Only then can relationships start to be what they are supposed to be. True love never seeks to be first or to be in control, but rather it takes the place of humble service. If my husband and I had kept this in our marriage, we would be sitting next to the King now, and this great hall would be filled with many more souls."

Removing More Veils

With that, the Reformer's wife disappeared back into the ranks of the glorified saints. I looked again toward the throne and was taken aback because the glory appeared so much more beautiful than it had before. Another man standing close to me explained.

"With each encounter, a veil is being removed so that you can see Him more clearly. You are not changed just by seeing His glory, but by seeing it with an unveiled face. Those who come to the true judgments of God walk a corridor such as this to meet those who can help them remove whatever veils they are still wearing—veils that will distort their vision of Him."

I felt that I had already absorbed more understanding than my many years of ministry on earth had given me. All my study and seeking on earth had apparently only led me forward at a snail's pace. Even *many* lifetimes would not have prepared me to face the judgment! My life had already disqualified me more than all those I had met, and it seemed they had barely made it here!

"How could those who have not been given the grace of this experience have any hope at all?" I asked.

I heard a new voice say, "What you are experiencing here has been given to you on earth. Every relationship, every encounter with another person, could teach you what you are learning here if you keep that cloak of humility on and learn to always keep your attention fixed on His glory. You are being given this experience now because you will write the vision, and those who read it will understand it. Many will then be able to carry the glory and the power that they will need in the last battle."

I was amazed to recognize this man as a contemporary of mine, for I did not even know he had died. I had never met him on earth, but he had a great ministry which I respected very much. Through men that he had trained, thousands had been led to salvation, and many large churches had been raised up that were almost totally devoted to evangelism.

He asked if he could just embrace me for a minute, and I agreed, feeling quite awkward. When we embraced, I felt such love coming from him that a great pain deep within me stopped hurting. I had become so used to the pain that I did not even notice it until it stopped. After he released me, I told him that his embrace had healed me of something. His joy at this was profound. Then he began to tell me why he was in the lowest rank in heaven.

"I became so proud near the end of my life that I could not imagine that the Lord would do anything of significance unless He did it through me. I began to touch the Lord's anointed and do His prophets harm. I was selfishly proud when the Lord used one of my own disciples, and I became jealous when the Lord moved through anyone who was outside of my ministry. I would search for anything that was wrong with them in order to expose them. I did not know that every time I did this I only demoted myself further."

"I never knew you had done anything like that," I said, surprised.

"I did not do it myself, but I incited men under me to investigate other ministers and do my dirty work. I had them scour the earth to find any error or sin in the lives of others so they could be exposed. I became the worst thing that a man can become on the earth—a stumbling block who produced other stumbling blocks. We sowed fear and division throughout the church, all in the name of protecting the truth. In my self-righteousness, I was headed for perdition.

"But in His great mercy, the Lord allowed me to be struck by a disease that would bring about a slow and humiliating death. Just before I died, I came to my senses and repented. I am thankful to be here at all. I may be one of the least of His here, but it is much more than I deserve.

I just could not leave this room until I had a chance to apologize to those of you that I so wronged."

"But you never wronged me," I said.

"Oh, but I did indeed," he replied. "Many of the attacks that came against you were from those I had agitated and encouraged in their assaults on others. Even though I may not have personally carried out the attacks, the Lord holds me as responsible as those who did."

"I see. Of course I forgive you."

Judging the Stumbling Blocks

I was already beginning to remember how I had done this same thing, even though on a smaller scale. I recalled how I had allowed disgruntled former members of a nearby church to spread their poison about that church without stopping them. By allowing them to do this without correcting them, I had, in effect, encouraged them to continue. At the time, I had rationalized that this was justified because of the errors of that church. I had even repeated many of their stories, justifying it under the guise of enlisting prayers for them.

Soon a great flood of memories of other such incidents began to arise in my heart. Again, I was starting to be overwhelmed by the evil and darkness of my own soul.

"I, too, have been a stumbling block!" I wailed. I knew that I deserved death and that I deserved the worst kind of hell. I had never seen such ruthlessness and cruelty as I was now seeing in my own heart.

"We actually comforted ourselves by thinking we were doing God a favor when we attacked His children," continued the understanding voice of this man. "It is good for you to see this here because you can go back. Please warn my disciples of their impending doom if they do not repent. Many of them are called to be kings here, but if they do not repent, they will face the worst judgment of all—the judgment of the stumbling blocks.

"My humbling disease was grace from God. When I stood before the throne, I asked the Lord to send such grace to my disciples. I cannot cross back over to them, but He has allowed me this time with you. Please forgive and release those who have attacked you. They really do not understand that they are doing the work of the accuser. Thank you for forgiving me, but please also forgive them. It is in your power to retain sins or to cover them with love. I entreat you to love those who are now your enemies."

I was so overwhelmed with my own sin that I could hardly hear this man. He was glorious and pure and obviously now had powers that were not known on the earth. Yet he was entreating me with great humility. I felt such love coming from him that I could not imagine refusing him. But even without the impact of his love, I felt far more guilty than anyone attacking me could possibly be.

"Certainly I must deserve anything they have done to me and much more," I replied.

"That is true, but it is not the point here," he entreated. "Everyone on earth is deserving of the second death, but our Savior brought us grace and truth. If we are to do His work, we must do everything in both grace and truth. Truth without grace is what the enemy brings when he comes as an 'angel of light.'"

"If I can be delivered from this, maybe I will be able to help them," I replied. "But can't you recognize that I am far worse than they could possibly be?"

"I know that what just passed through your memory was bad," he answered, with profound love and grace. I knew that he had now become as concerned for me and my condition as he had been for his own disciples.

"This really is heaven," I blurted out. "This really is light and truth. How could we who live in such darkness become so proud, thinking we know so much about God?" Impulsively, I yelled in the direction of the throne, "Lord! Please let me go and carry this light back to earth!"

Immediately, the entire host of heaven seemed to stand at attention, and I knew that I was the center of their gaze. I felt so insignificant before just one of these glorious ones, but when I knew they were *all* looking at me, fear came like a tidal wave. I felt there could be no doom like I was about to experience. Surely I was the greatest enemy of the glory and truth that so filled that place.

When I thought about my request to go back, I realized I was too depraved. I could never adequately represent such glory and truth. There was no way I could, in my corruption, convey the reality of that glorious place and His presence. I felt that even Satan had not fallen as far as I had. *This is hell!* I thought. There could be no worse pain than to be as evil as I was and to know that this kind of glory existed. To be banned from here would be a torture worse than I ever feared. "No wonder the demons are so angry and demented," I said under my breath.

Just when I felt that I was about to be banished to the deepest regions of hell, I simply cried, "JESUS!" Immediately, a deep peace came over me. I knew I had to move on toward the glory again, and somehow I had the confidence to do it.

The Writer's Remorse

I kept moving until I saw a man I considered to be one of the greatest writers of all time. I had counted his insights into the truth to be possibly the greatest I had encountered in all my studies.

"Sir, I have always looked forward to this meeting," I blurted out.

"As have I," he replied with genuine sincerity.

I was surprised by his comment, but I was so excited to meet him that I continued, "I feel that I know you, and in your writings I felt like you somehow knew me. I think I owe more to you than to anyone else who was not canonized in Scripture."

"You are very gracious," he replied. "But I am sorry that I did not serve you better. I was a shallow person, and my writings were shallow, filled more with worldly wisdom than divine truth."

"I know what you are saying must be true because you can only speak the truth here," I told him. "Yet it is hard for me to understand. I think your writings are some of the best that we have on earth."

"You are right," this famous writer admitted with sincerity. "It is so sad. Everyone here, even those who sit closest to the King, would live their lives differently if they had them to live over. But I think I would live mine even more differently than most. I was honored by kings, but failed the King of kings. I used the great gifts and insights that were given to me to draw men more to myself and my wisdom than to Him. Besides, I only knew Him by the hearing of the ear, which is the way I compelled other men to know Him. I made them dependent on me and on others like me. I turned them more to deductive reasoning than to the Holy Spirit, whom I hardly knew.

"I did not point men to Jesus," he continued, "but to myself and others like me who pretended to know Him. When I beheld Him here, I wanted to grind my writings into powder, just as Moses did with the golden calf. My mind was my idol, and I wanted everyone to worship my mind with me.

"Your esteem for me does not cause me to rejoice. If I had spent as much time seeking to know Him as I did seeking to know *about* Him in order to impress others with my knowledge, many of those who are in this lowest of companies would be sitting in the thrones that were prepared for them, and many others would be in this room."

"I know what you are saying about your work must be true, but aren't you being a little too hard on yourself?" I questioned. "Your works fed me spiritually for many years, as I know they have multitudes of others."

"I am not being too hard on myself," he responded. "All that I have said is true, and it was confirmed when I stood before the throne. Even though I produced a lot, I was given more talents than almost anyone here, and I buried them beneath my own spiritual pride and ambitions. Just as we learn from the example of Adam, who could have carried the whole human race into a most glorious future, but by his failure led billions of souls into the worst of dooms instead—with authority comes responsibility.

"The more authority you are given, the more potential for both good and evil you have. Those who will rule with Him for the ages will know responsibility of the most profound kind. No man stands alone, and every human failure or victory resonates far beyond our comprehension, even to generations to come."

I could not help reflecting on the beautiful and articulate phrases that this man had written. He was the epitome of a wordsmith, a craftsman who turned words into works of art. But here, he was speaking as a common man, without the flair for which his writings were so well-known. Although he knew what I was thinking, as did everyone here, he continued with what he clearly thought was more important.

"Had I sought the Lord Himself instead of knowledge about Him, I could have successfully led many thousands, which would have resulted in many more millions being here now. Anyone who understands the true nature of authority would never seek it. They would only accept it when they knew they were yoked with the Lord, the only One who can carry authority without stumbling. Never seek influence for yourself, but only seek the Lord and be willing to take His yoke. My influence did not feed your heart, but rather your pride in knowledge."

"How can I know that I am not doing the same?" I asked as I began to think of my own writings.

"Study to show yourself approved unto God, not men," he replied as he walked back into the ranks. Before disappearing he turned, and with the slightest smile offered one last bit of advice: "And do not follow me."

Higher Ranks

In this first multitude I saw many other men and women of God, both from history and from my own time. I stopped and talked to many of them, and was shocked that so many I expected to be in the highest positions were instead in the lowest rank of the kingdom. Many shared the same basic story—they had fallen to the deadly sin of pride after their great victories, or jealousy when other men were anointed as much as they were. Others had fallen to lust, discouragement, or bitterness near the end of their lives and had to be taken before they crossed the line into perdition. They all gave me the same warning: The higher the spiritual authority that you walk in, the further you can fall if you are without love and humility.

As I continued toward the judgment seat, I began to pass those who were of higher rank in the kingdom. After many more veils had been stripped away from me by meetings with those who had stumbled over the same problems that I had, I began to meet some who had overcome. I met couples who had served God and each other faithfully to the end. Their glory here was unspeakable, and their victory encouraged me that it was possible to stay on the path of life and serve the Lord faithfully.

Those who stumbled did so in many different ways. But those who prevailed all did it the same way: They did not deviate from their devotion to the first and greatest commandment—loving the Lord. In this way, their service was done unto Him, not to men. These were the ones who worshiped the Lamb and followed Him wherever He went.

When I was still not even halfway to the throne, what had been the indescribable glory of the first rank now seemed to be outer darkness in comparison to the glory of those I was now passing. The greatest beauty on earth would not qualify to be found anywhere in heaven. And I was told that this room was just the *threshold* of indescribable realms of glory!

My march to the throne may have taken days, months, or even years. There was no way to measure time in that place. Everyone there showed respect to me, not because of who I was or anything I had done, but simply because I was a warrior in the battle of the last days. Somehow, through this last battle, the glory of God was to be revealed in such a way that it would be a witness to every power and authority, created or yet to be created, for all of eternity. During this battle, the glory of the cross would be revealed, and the wisdom of God would be known in a special way. To be in that battle was to be given one of the greatest honors possible.

Near the judgment seat of Christ, those in the highest ranks were sitting on thrones that were all a part of His throne. Even the least of these thrones was many times more glorious than any earthly throne. Some of those on the thrones were rulers over cities on earth and would soon take their places. Others were rulers over the affairs of heaven, and still others ruled over the affairs of the physical creation, such as star systems and galaxies.

It was apparent that those who were given authority over cities were esteemed, even above those who had been given authority over galaxies. The value of a single child surpasses that of a galaxy of stars because the Lord has chosen men as His eternal dwelling place. In the presence of His glory, the whole earth seemed as insignificant as a speck of dust. Yet it was so infinitely esteemed that all of creation's attention was upon it.

His Awesome Presence

Now that I stood before the throne, I felt even lower than a speck of dust. Nevertheless, I felt the Holy Spirit upon me in a greater way than I ever had. It was by His power alone that I was able to stand. It was here that I truly came to understand His ministry as the Comforter. He had led me through the entire journey, even though for the most part I had been unaware of His presence.

The Lord was both more gentle and more terrible than I had ever imagined. In Him I saw Wisdom, who had accompanied me on the mountain. I somehow also felt the familiarity of many of my friends on earth, which I understood to be because He had often spoken to me through them. I also recognized Him as the One I had often rejected when He had come to me in others. I saw both a Lion and a Lamb, the Shepherd and the Bridegroom, but most of all I now saw Him as the Judge.

Even in the Lord's awesome presence, the Comforter was so mightily with me that I was comfortable. It was clear that the Lord in no way wanted me to be uncomfortable; He only wanted me to know the truth. Human words are not adequate to describe how awesome or how relieving it was to stand before Him. I had passed the point where I was concerned if the judgment was going to be good or bad; I just knew it would be right and that I could trust my Judge.

At one point the Lord looked toward the galleries of thrones around Him. Many were occupied, but many were empty. He then said, *"These thrones are for the overcomers who have served Me faithfully in every generation. My Father and I prepared them before the foundation of the world. Are you worthy to sit on one of these?"*

I remembered what a friend had once said, "When the omniscient God asks you a question, it is not because He is seeking information." I looked at those who were now seated on the thrones. I could recognize some of the great heroes of the faith, but realized most of those seated had not even been well-known on earth.

Many of those on the thrones had been missionaries who expended their lives in obscurity. They had never cared to be remembered on earth, but wanted only to be remembered by Him. I was a bit surprised to see some who had been wealthy, and rulers who had been faithful with what they had been given. However, it seemed that faithful, praying women and mothers occupied more thrones than any other single group.

There was no way I could answer "yes" to the Lord's question regarding whether I considered myself worthy to sit here. I was not worthy to sit in the company of any who were there. I knew I had been given the opportunity to run for the greatest prize in heaven or earth, and I had failed. I was desperate, but there was still one hope. Even though most of my life had been a failure, I was very glad that I was here before finishing my life on earth.

When I confessed that I was not worthy, the Lord asked, *"But do you want this seat?"*

"I do with all of my heart," I responded.

The Lord then looked at the galleries and said, *"Those empty seats could have been filled in any generation. I gave the invitation to sit here to everyone who has called upon My name. The seats are still available. Now the last battle has come, and many who are last shall be first. These seats will be filled before the battle is over. Those who will sit here will be known by two things: They will wear the mantle of humility, and they will have My likeness.*

"You now have the mantle. If you can keep it and do not lose it in the battle, when you return you will also have My likeness. Then you will be worthy to sit with these because I will have made you worthy. All authority and power have been given to Me, and I alone can wield it. You will prevail, and you will be trusted with My authority only when you have come to fully abide in Me. Now turn and look at My household."

I turned and looked back in the direction I had come from. Standing before His throne, I could see the entire room. The spectacle was glorious beyond description. Millions filled the ranks. Each individual in the lowest rank was more awesome than any army and had more power. It was far beyond my capacity to absorb such a panorama of glory. Even so, I could see that only a very small portion of the great room was occupied.

The Cup of Tears

I then looked back at the Lord and was astonished to see tears in His eyes. He had wiped the tears away from every eye here except His own. As a tear ran down His cheek, He caught it in His hand. He then offered it to me.

"This is My cup. Will you drink it with Me?"

There was no way I could refuse Him. As the Lord continued to look at me, I began to feel His great love. Even as foul as I was, He still loved me. As undeserving as I was, He wanted me to be close to Him. Then He said:

"I love all of these with a love that you cannot now understand. I also love all who were supposed to be here but did not come. I left the ninety-nine to go after the one who was lost.

My shepherds will not leave the one to go after the ninety-nine who are still lost. I came to save the lost. Will you share My heart to go and save the lost? Will you help to fill this room? Will you help to fill these thrones and every other seat in this hall? Will you take up this quest to bring joy to heaven, to Me, and to My Father?

"*This is judgment for My own household, and My own house is not full. The last battle will not be over until My house is full. Only then will it be time for us to redeem the earth and remove the evil from My creation. If you drink My cup, you will love the lost the way that I love them.*"

He took a cup so plain that it seemed out of place in a room of such glory, and He placed His tear in it. He then gave it to me. I have never tasted anything so bitter! I knew that I could in no way drink it all, or even much of it, but I was determined to drink as much as I could. The Lord patiently waited until I finally erupted into such weeping that I felt like rivers of tears were flowing from me. I was crying for the lost, but even more, I was crying for the Lord.

I looked to Him in desperation, for I could not take any more of the great pain. Then His peace began to fill me, flowing together with the river of His love that erupted when I drank from His cup. Never had I felt anything so wonderful. This was the living water that I knew would spring up for eternity.

Then I felt as if the waters flowing within me caught on fire! I began to feel that this fire would consume me if I could not start declaring the majesty of His glory. I had never felt such an urge to preach, to worship Him, and to breathe every breath for the sake of His gospel.

"Lord!" I shouted, forgetting everyone but Him. "I now know that this throne of judgment is also the throne of grace, and I ask You now for the grace to serve You. Above all things, I ask You for grace! I ask You for the grace to finish my course. I ask You for the grace to love You like this, so I can be delivered from the delusions and self-centeredness that have so perverted my life.

"I call upon You for salvation from myself and the evil of my heart, so this love I now feel can flow in my heart continually. I ask You to give me Your heart, Your love. I ask for the grace of the Holy Spirit to convict me of my sin and to testify of You as You really are. Give me the grace to preach the reality of this judgment and testify of all You have prepared for those who come to You. I ask for the grace to share with those who are called to occupy these empty thrones, to give them words of encouragement that will keep them on the path of life and impart to them the faith to do what they have been called to do. Lord, I beg You for this grace!"

Commissioned

The Lord then stood up, and all those who were seated upon the thrones for as far as I could see also stood up. His eyes burned with a fire I had not seen before.

"You have called upon Me for grace. This request I never deny. You shall return, and the Holy Spirit shall be with you. Here you have tasted of both My kindness and My severity. You

must remember both if you are to stay on the path of life. The true love of God includes the judgment of God. You must know both My kindness and severity or you will fall to deception. This is the grace that you have been given here, to know both. The conversations you had with your brethren here were My grace. Remember them."

He pointed His sword toward my heart, then my mouth, then my hands. When He did, fire came from His sword and burned me. The pain was very great. "This, too, is grace," He said. "You are but one of many who have been prepared for this hour. Preach and write about all that you have seen here. What I have said to you, say to My brethren.

"Go and call My captains to the last battle. Go and defend the poor and the oppressed, the widows and the orphans. This is the commission of My captains, and it is where you will find them. My children are worth more to Me than the stars in the heavens. Feed My lambs. Watch over My little ones. Give the Word of God to them that they may live. Go to the battle. Go and do not retreat. Go quickly, for I will come quickly. Obey Me and hasten the day of My coming."

A company of angels then came and escorted me away from the throne. The leader walked beside me and began to speak.

"Now that He has stood, He will not sit again until the last battle is over. He has been seated until the time when His enemies are to be put under His feet. The time has now come. The legions of angels that have been standing ready since the night of His passion have now been released upon the earth. The hordes of hell have also been released.

The White Throne

"This is the time for which all of creation has been waiting," he continued. "The great mystery of God will soon be finished. We will now fight until the end. We will fight alongside you and your brethren."

The Final Quest

Part V

THE OVERCOMERS

As I continued walking away from the judgment seat, I began to reflect on all that I had just experienced. It had been both terrible and wonderful. As challenging and heartrending as it had been, I felt more secure than I ever had. At first, it had not been easy to be stripped so bare in front of so many, unable to hide even a single thought. But when I just relaxed and accepted it, knowing that it was cleansing my very soul, it became profoundly liberating. Having nothing to hide was like casting off the heaviest yoke and the strongest shackles. I began to feel as if I could breathe like I had never breathed before.

The more at ease I became, the more my mind seemed to increase in its capacity. Then I began to sense a communication going on which no human words could articulate. I thought of the Apostle Paul's comments about his visit to the third heaven, where he had heard inexpressible words—a spiritual communication that greatly transcends any form of human communication. It is more profound and meaningful than human words are able to convey. Somehow it is a pure communication of the heart and mind together, so pure that there is no possibility of misunderstanding.

As I looked at someone in the room, I began to understand what he was thinking, just as he had been able to understand me. When I looked at the Lord, I began to understand Him in the same way. We contin-ued to use words, but the meaning of each one had a depth that no dictionary could have ever captured. My mind had been freed so that its capacity was multiplied many times over. It was exhilarating beyond any previous experience.

The Spirit's Communication

It was also obvious that the Lord was enjoying being able to communicate this way with me as much as I was with Him. Never before had I understood so deeply what it meant for Him to be the Word of God. Jesus is the Communication of God to His creation. His words are spirit and life, and their meaning and power greatly exceed our present human definitions.

Human words are a very superficial form of the communication of the Spirit. God created us with the ability to communicate on a level that far transcends human words, but because of the Fall and the debacle at the Tower of Babel, we lost this capacity. We cannot be who we were created to be until we regain this, and we can only attain it when we are freed in His presence.

I began to understand that when Adam's transgression caused him to hide from God, it was the beginning of a most terrible distortion of what man was created to be. It brought about a severe reduction of our intellectual and spiritual capacities. These can only be restored when we "come out of hiding" and are genuinely transparent. This means opening ourselves to God and to each other. It is as we behold the glory of the Lord with an "unveiled face" that we are changed into His image. The veils, caused by our hiding, must be discarded.

The Lord's first question to Adam after his transgression was, "Where are you?" In the same way, it is the first question that we must answer if we are to be fully restored to Him. Of course, the Lord knew where Adam was. The question was for Adam's sake. That question was the beginning of God's quest for man.

The story of redemption is God's pursuit of man, not man's pursuit of God. When we can fully answer this question, knowing where we are in relation to God, we will have been fully restored to Him. But we can only know the answer to this question when we are in His presence.

That was the essence of my entire experience at the judgment seat. The Lord already knew all there was to know about me. The whole experience was for my sake, so I would know where I was. It was all to bring me out of hiding, to bring me out of darkness and into the light.

I also began to understand just how much the Lord desired to be one with His people. Through the entire judgment, He was not trying to get me to see something as good or bad as much as to see it in union with Him. The Lord was seeking me more than I was seeking Him. His judgments set me free, and His judgment of the world will set the world free.

The darkness in the world has been perpetuated by our compulsion to hide, which began immediately after the Fall. "Walking in the light" is more than just knowing and obeying certain truths—it is *being* true and being free from the compulsion to hide. When judgment day comes, it will bring the final deliverance of Adam from his hiding place. Not only will it be the final liberation of Adam, but it will also begin the final liberation of the creation, which was subject to bondage because of Adam.

"Walking in the light" means no more hiding from God or anyone else. The nakedness of Adam and Eve before the Fall was not just physical, but spiritual as well. When our salvation is complete, we will know this kind of transparency again. To be completely open to others will unlock realms we do not presently even know exist. This is what Satan is attempting to counterfeit through the New Age movement.

Wisdom Returns

As I walked, pondering all that I had learned, the Lord suddenly appeared by my side again in the form of Wisdom. He now appeared far more glorious than I had ever seen Him, even when He was on the judgment seat. I was both stunned and overjoyed.

"Lord, are You returning with me like this?" I asked.

"I will always be with you like this. However, I want to be even more to you than the way you see Me now. You have seen My kindness and My severity here, but you still do not fully know Me as the Righteous Judge."

This surprised me. I had just spent a considerable amount of time before His judgment seat and felt that all I had been learning pertained to His judgment. He paused to let this sink in, and then continued.

"There is a freedom that comes when you perceive truth, but whomever I set free is free indeed. The freedom of My presence is greater than just knowing truth. You have experienced liberation in My presence, but there is yet much more for you to understand about My judgments. When I judge, I am not seeking to condemn or to justify, but to bring forth righteousness. Righteousness is only found in union with Me. That is the righteous judgment—bringing men into unity with Me.

"My church is now clothed with shame because she does not have judges. She does not have judges because she does not know Me as the Judge. I will now raise up judges for My people who know My judgment. They will not only decide between people or issues; they will make things right, which means bringing them into agreement with Me.

"When I appeared to Joshua as the Captain of the Host, I declared that I was neither for him nor his enemies. I never come to take sides. When I come, it is to take over—not to take sides. I appeared as the Captain of the Host before Israel could enter her Promised Land. The church is now about to enter her Promised Land, and I am again about to appear as the Captain

of the Host. When I do, I will remove all who have been forcing My people to take sides against their brothers.

"My justice does not take sides in human conflicts, even those involving My people. What I was doing through Israel, I was doing for their enemies, too—not against them. It is only because you see from the earthly, temporal perspective that you do not see My justice. You must see My justice in order to walk in My authority because righteousness and justice are the foundation of My throne.

"I have imputed righteousness to the people I have chosen. But like Israel in the wilderness, even the greatest saints of the church age have only aligned themselves with My ways a small portion of the time, or with a small part of their minds and hearts. I am not for them or against their enemies, but I am coming to use My people to save their enemies. I love all men and desire for all to be saved."

Brethren Used by the Enemy

I could not help thinking about the great battle we had fought on the mountain. We had wounded many of our own brethren as we fought against the evil controlling them. Many of them were still in the camp of the enemy, either being used by him or kept as his prisoners. I started to wonder if the next battle would be against our own brothers again. The Lord was watching me ponder all of this, and then He continued.

"Until the last battle is over, there will always be some of our brothers who are being used by the enemy. But that is not why I am telling you this now. I am telling you this to help you see

how the enemy gets into your own heart and mind, and how he uses you! Even now, you still do not see everything the way I do.

"This is common with My people. At this time, even My greatest leaders are seldom in harmony with Me. Many are doing good works, but very few are doing what I have called them to do. This is largely the result of divisions among you. I am not coming to take sides with any one group, but I am calling for those who will come over to My side.

"You are impressed when I give you a 'word of knowledge' about someone's physical illness, or some other knowledge that is not known to you. This knowledge comes when you touch My mind to just a small degree. I know all things. If you were to fully have My mind, you would be able to know everything about everyone you encounter, just as you have begun to experience here. You would see all men just the way I see them. But even then, there is more to fully abiding in Me. To know how to use such knowledge rightly, you must have My heart. Only then will you have My judgment.

"I can only trust you with My supernatural knowledge to the degree that you know My heart. The gifts of the Spirit that I have released to My church are but small tokens of the powers of the age to come. I have called you to be messengers of that age, and you must therefore know its powers. You should earnestly desire the gifts because they are a part of Me, and I have given them to you so that you can be like Me. You are right to seek to know My mind, My ways, and My purposes, but you must also earnestly desire to know My heart. When you know My heart, then the eyes of your heart will be opened. Then you will see as I see, and you will do what I do.

"I am about to entrust much more of the powers of the age to come to My church. However, there is a great deception that often comes upon those who are trusted with great power. If you do not understand what I am about to show you, you too will fall to this deception.

"You have asked for My grace, and you shall have it. The first grace that will keep you on the path of life is to know the level of your present deception. Deception involves anything that you do not understand as I do. Knowing the level of your present deception brings humility, and I give My grace to the humble.

"That is why I said, 'Who is blind but My servant?' And that is why I told the Pharisees, 'It is for judgment that I came into the world . . . to give sight to those who do not see and to make blind those who see . . . If you were blind you would not be guilty, but because you claim to see, your guilt remains.' That is also why My light struck Paul blind when I called him. My light only revealed his true condition. Like him, you must be struck blind in the natural so that you can see by My Spirit."

The Apostle's Advice

I felt compelled to look at those who were sitting on the thrones we were passing. As I did, my gaze fell upon a man I knew was the Apostle Paul. As I looked back at the Lord, He motioned for me to speak to him.

"I have so looked forward to this," I said, feeling awkward but excited by this meeting. "I know you are aware of how much your letters have guided the church, and they are probably still accomplishing more than all the rest of us put together. You are still one of the greatest lights on earth."

"Thank you," he said graciously. "But you do not understand just how much we have looked forward to meeting all of you. You are soldiers in the last battle; you are the ones everyone here is waiting to meet. We only saw these days dimly through our limited prophetic vision, but you have been chosen to live in them. You are soldiers preparing for the last battle. You are the ones we have all been waiting for."

Still feeling awkward, I continued, "But there is no way that I can convey the appreciation we feel for you and for the others who helped set our course with their lives and their writings. I also know we will have an eternity for exchanging our appreciation, so please, while I am here, let me ask: What would you say to my generation that will help us in this battle?"

"I can only say to you now what I have already said to you through my writings," Paul stated, looking me resolutely in the eyes. "However, you will understand them better if you realize that I fell short of all that I was called to do."

"But you are here, on one of the greatest thrones!" I protested. "You are still reaping more fruit for eternal life than any of us could ever hope to reap."

"By the grace of God I was able to finish my course, but I still did not walk in all that I was called to. I fell short of the highest purposes that I could have walked in—everyone has. I know that some would practically consider it blasphemy to think of me as anything less than the greatest example of Christian ministry, yet I was being honest when I wrote near the end of my life that I was the greatest of sinners. I was not saying that I *had been* the greatest of sinners, but rather that I was the greatest of sinners *then*. Even though I had been given so much understanding, I walked in comparatively little of it."

"How could that possibly be?" I asked. "I thought you were just being humble."

"True humility is agreement with the truth. Do not fear. My letters were true, and they were written by the anointing of the Holy Spirit. However, I was given so much, and I did not use all that I was given. I, too, fell short. Everyone here has fallen short, except One. The reason you particularly must see this about me is that many are still distorting my teachings because they have a distorted view of me.

"As you saw the progression in my letters, I went from feeling that I was not inferior to even the most eminent apostles to acknowledging that I was the least of the apostles. I then saw that I was the least of the saints, and finally that I was the greatest of sinners. I was not just being humble; I was speaking sober truth. I was entrusted with much more than I used. Only One here fully believed, fully obeyed, and truly finished all that He was given to do. But you can walk in much more than I did."

Rediscovering the Foundation

Rather feebly, I replied, "I know what you are saying is true, but are you sure this is the most important message you could give to us for the last battle?"

"I am sure!" he replied with utter conviction. "I so appreciate the grace of the Lord to use my letters as He has, but I am concerned with the way many of you are using them improperly. They are the truth of the Holy Spirit and they are Scripture. The Lord did give me great stones to set into the structure of His eternal church, but they are not foundation stones. The foundation stones were laid by Jesus alone. My life and ministry are not the example of what you are called to be; Jesus alone is that.

"If what I have written is used as a foundation, it will not be able to hold the weight of that which needs to be built upon it. What I have written must be built upon the only Foundation that can withstand what you are about to endure; it must not be used as the foundation. You must see my teachings through the Lord's teachings, not try to understand Him from my perspective. His Words are the foundation. I have only built upon them by elaborating on His Words. The greatest wisdom and the most powerful truths are His Words, not mine.

"It is important for you to know that I did not walk in all that was available to me. There is much more available for every believer to walk in than I did. All true believers have the Holy Spirit in them. The power of the One who created all things lives within them. The least of the saints has the power to move mountains, to stop armies, or to raise the dead.

"If you are to accomplish all that you are called to do in your day, my ministry must not be viewed as the ultimate, but merely as a starting place. Your goal must not be to be like me, but to be like the Lord. You can be like Him and do everything that He did, and even more, because He saved His best wine for last."

I reminded myself that only truth could be spoken here. I knew that Paul was right concerning the wrong use of his teachings as a foundation, rather than building upon the foundation of the Gospels. But it was still hard for me to accept that Paul had fallen short of his calling.

I looked at Paul's throne and the glory of his being. It was much more than I ever dreamed the greatest saints in heaven would have. He was every bit as forthright and resolute as I had expected him to be. It struck me how obvious it was that he still carried his great concern for all of the churches. I had idolized him, and that was a transgression he was trying to set me free from. Even so, he was much greater than the Paul I had idolized. Knowing what I was thinking, he put both hands on my shoulders and looked at me even more resolutely in the eyes.

"I am your brother. I love you as everyone here does. But you must understand that our course is now finished. We can neither add to nor take away from what we planted on the earth, but you can. We are not your hope. You are now *our* hope. Even in this conversation I can only confirm what I have already written, but you still have much writing to do. Worship only God, and grow up in all things into Him. Never make any man your goal, but only Him.

"Many will soon walk the earth who will do much greater works than we did. The first shall be last, and the last, first. We do not mind this. It is the joy of our hearts because we are one with you. The Lord used my generation to lay and begin building upon the foundation, and we will always have the honor of participating in that. But every floor built upon the foundation should go higher. We will not be the building we are supposed to be unless you go higher."

The Ministry and the Message

As I pondered this, he watched me closely. Then he continued, "There are two things we attained in our time that were lost very quickly by the church. They have not yet been recovered, but you must recover them."

"What are they?" I inquired, feeling that what he was about to say was more than just an addendum to what he had already shared with me.

"You must recover the *ministry* and the *message*," he said emphatically.

I looked at the Lord, and He nodded His affirmation, adding, *"It is right that Paul should say this to you. Until this time he has been the most faithful with both of these."*

"Please explain," I implored Paul.

"All right," he replied. "Except for a few places in the world where there are great persecutions or difficulties, we can hardly recognize either the ministry or the message that is being preached today. Therefore, the church is now but a phantom of what it was even in our time, and we were far from all we were called to be. When we served, being in ministry was the greatest sacrifice that one could make, and this reflected the message of the greatest sacrifice that was made—the cross.

"The cross is the power of God, and it is the center of all we are called to live by. You now have so little power to transform the minds and hearts of believers because you do not live or preach the cross. Therefore, we have difficulty seeing much difference between the church and the heathen. That is not the gospel or the salvation that we were entrusted with. You must return to the cross."

With those words, he squeezed my shoulders like a father and then returned to his seat. I felt as if I had received both an incredible blessing and a profound rebuke. As I walked away, I began thinking about the level of Salvation on the mountain, and the treasures of salvation I had seen inside the mountain. I began to see that most of my own decisions—even the decision to enter the door that led me here—were based mainly on what would get me further, not on a consideration of the will of the Lord.

I was still living for myself, not for Him. Even in my desire to embrace the judgments here, I was motivated by what would help me make it back in victory without suffering loss. I was still walking much more in self-centeredness than in Christ-centeredness.

The Last-Day Church

I knew the short talk with Paul would have consequences that would take a long time to fully understand. In a way, I felt that I had received a blessing from the entire eternal church. We really were being cheered on by the great cloud of witnesses. They looked at us like proud parents who wanted better things for their children than they themselves had known. Their greatest joy would be to see the church in the last days become everything the church in their day had failed to attain. I also knew I was still falling far short of what they had prepared for us to walk in.

"The last-day church will not be greater than Paul's generation, even if she does greater works," the Lord interjected. *"All that is done is done by My grace. However, I will make more of My grace and power available to the last-day church because she must accomplish more than the church in any age has yet accomplished.*

"Last-day believers will walk in all the power that I demonstrated, and more, because they will be the final representatives of all who have gone before them. The church will demonstrate My nature and My ways as they have never been demonstrated before by men. It is because I am giving you more grace, and to whom much is given much will be required."

This just made me think even more about Paul. "How could we even become as dedicated and faithful as he was?" I thought to myself.

"I am not asking you to attain that," the Lord answered. *"I am asking you to abide in Me. You cannot continue to measure yourself by others—not even Paul. You will always fall short of the one you look to, but if you are looking to Me you will go far beyond what you would have otherwise accomplished. As you yourself have taught, it was when the two on the road to Emmaus saw Me break the bread that their eyes were opened. When you read Paul's letters, or anyone else's writings, you must hear Me. Only when you receive your bread directly from Me will the eyes of your heart be opened.*

"You can be distracted the most by those who are the most like Me if you do not see through them to see Me. There is also another trap for those who come to know more of My anointing and power than others. They are often distracted by looking at themselves. As I was saying before you talked to Paul, My servants must become blind so that they can see. I let you talk to him then because he is one of My best examples of this. It was because of My grace that I allowed him to persecute My church. When he saw My light, he understood that his own reasoning had led him into direct conflict with the very truth he claimed to be serving.

"Your reasoning will always do that. It will lead you to do that which is exactly contrary to My will. Greater anointing brings greater danger of this happening to you, if you do not learn what Paul did. If you do not take up your cross every day, laying down all that you are and all that you have before it, you will fall because of the authority and power that I will give you. Until you learn to do all things for the sake of the gospel, the more influence you have, the greater the danger of this you will face.

"Sometimes My anointed ones are deceived into thinking that because I give them a little supernatural knowledge or power, their ways must therefore be My ways and everything they think must be what I think. This is a great deception, and many have stumbled because of it. You think like Me when you are in perfect union with Me. Even with the most anointed who have yet walked the earth, such as Paul, this union has only been partial and for brief periods of time.

"Paul walked with Me as close as any man ever has. Even so, he was also beset by fears and weaknesses that were not from

Me. I could have delivered him from these, as he requested several times, but I had a reason for not delivering him. Paul's great wisdom was to embrace his weaknesses, understanding that if I had delivered him from them, I would not have been able to trust him with the level of revelation and power that I did.

"Paul recognized his own weaknesses and learned to distinguish between them and the revelation of My Spirit. When he was beset with weakness or fear, he knew he was not seeing from My perspective, but from his own. This caused him to seek Me and depend on Me even more. He was also careful not to confuse what came from his own mind and heart with the thoughts of My mind and heart. Therefore I could trust him with revelations that I could not entrust to others."

The Quest

I began to think about how clear all of this was here, but how very often, even after I have had a great experience like this, I still forget it so easily. It is easy to understand and to walk in the light here, but back in the battle it becomes cloudy again. I also thought about how I was not so much beset with fears, as Paul was, but my tendencies were impatience and anger, which were just as much a distortion of the perspective we should have by abiding in the Holy Spirit.

Wisdom stopped and turned to me. *"You are an earthen vessel, and that is all you will be while you walk the earth. However, you can see Me just as clearly there as you do here, if you will look with the eyes of your heart. You can be just as close to Me there as anyone has ever been to Me, and even more so.*

"I have made the way for everyone to be as close to Me as they truly desire to be. If you really desire to be even closer to Me than Paul was, you can. Some will want this, and they will want it badly enough to give themselves fully to it, laying aside anything that hinders their intimacy with Me. They will have what they seek.

"If it is your quest to walk on earth just as you can walk with Me here, I will be just as close to you there as I am now. If you seek Me, you will find Me. If you draw near to Me, I will draw near to you. It is My desire to set a table for you right in the midst of your enemies. This is not just My desire for My leaders, but for all who call upon My name. I want to be much closer to you and to everyone who calls upon Me than I have yet been able to be with anyone who has lived on earth. You determine how close we will be, not I. I will be found by those who seek Me.

"You are here because you asked for My judgment in your life. You sought Me as the Judge, and now you are finding Me. But you must not think that just because you have seen My judgment seat, now all of your judgments will be My judgments. You will only have My judgments as you walk in unity with Me and seek the anointing of My Spirit. This can be gained or lost every day.

"I have let you see angels and given you many dreams and visions because you kept asking for them. I love to give My children the good gifts that they ask for. For years you asked Me for wisdom, so you are receiving it. You have asked Me to judge you, so you are receiving My judgment. But these experiences do *not make you fully wise, nor do they make you a righteous judge. You will only have wisdom and judgment as you abide in Me.*

"Do not ever stop seeking Me. The more you mature, the more you will know your desperate need for Me. The more you mature, the less you will seek to hide from Me or others for your desire will be to always walk in the light.

"You have seen Me as Savior, Lord, Wisdom, and Judge. When you return to the battle, you can still see My judgment seat with the eyes of your heart. When you walk in the knowledge that all you think and do are fully revealed here, you will have the freedom to live there just as you do here. It is only when you hide from Me or others that the veils return to hide Me from you. I am Truth, and those who worship Me must do so in Spirit and Truth.

"Truth is never found hiding in the darkness, but always seeks to remain in the light. Light exposes and makes manifest. Only when you seek to be exposed, and allow who you are in your heart to be exposed, will you walk in the light as I am in the light. True fellowship with Me requires complete exposure. True fellowship with My people requires the same.

"When you stood before the judgment seat, you felt more freedom and security than you have ever felt because you did not have to hide anymore. You felt more security because you knew that My judgments were true and righteous. The moral and spiritual order of My universe is just as sure as the natural order established upon the natural laws. You trust My law of gravity without even thinking about it. You must learn to trust My judgments in the same way. My standards of righteousness

are unchanging and are just as sure. To live by this truth is to walk in faith. True faith is to have confidence in who I am."

The Power of His Word

"You seek to know and walk in My power so that you can heal the sick and perform miracles, but you have not even begun to comprehend the power of My Word. To resurrect all the dead who have ever lived on earth will not even cause Me to strain. I uphold all things by the power of My Word. The creation exists because of My Word, and it is held together by My Word.

"Before the end, I will reveal My power on earth. Even so, the greatest power that I have ever revealed on the earth, or ever will, is still a very small demonstration of My power. I do not reveal My power to cause men to believe in My power, but to cause men to believe in My love.

"If I had wanted to save the world with My power when I walked the earth, I could have moved mountains by pointing a finger. Then all men would have bowed to Me, not because they loved Me or loved the truth, but because they feared My power. I do not want men to obey Me because they fear My power, but because they love Me and love the truth.

"If you do not know My love, then My power will corrupt you. I do not give you love so you can know My power, but I give you power so you can know My love. The goal of your life must be love, not power. Then I will give you power with which to love people. I will give you the power to heal the sick because you love them, and I love them, and I do not want them sick.

"So you must seek love first, and then faith. You cannot please Me without faith. But faith is not just the knowledge of

My power; it is the knowledge of My love and the power of My love. Faith must first be exercised in order to receive more love. Seek faith to love more and to do more with your love. Only when you seek the faith to love can I trust you with My power. Faith works by love.

"*My Word is the power that upholds all things. To the degree that you believe My Word is true, you can do all things. Those who really believe that My Words are true will also be true to their own words. It is My nature to be true, and the creation trusts My Word because I am faithful to it.*

"*Those who are like Me are also true to their own words. Their word is sure, and their commitments are trustworthy. Their 'yes' means 'yes,' and their 'no' means 'no.' If your own words are not true, you will also begin to doubt My Words because deception is in your heart. If you are not faithful to your own words, it is because you do not really know Me. To have faith, you must be faithful. I have called you to walk by faith because I am faithful. It is My nature.*

"*That is why you will be judged because of the careless words you speak. To be careless is to care less. Words have power, and those who are careless with words cannot be trusted with the power of My Word. It is wisdom to be careful with your words and to keep them as I do Mine.*"

The Lord's words were rolling over me like great waves from the sea. I felt like Job before the whirlwind. I thought that I was getting smaller and smaller and then realized that He was getting larger. I had never felt so presumptuous. How could I have been so casual with God? I felt like an ant staring up at a mountain range. I was less than dust, yet He was taking the time to speak to me. I could not stand it any more and turned away.

After a few moments, I felt a reassuring hand on my shoulder. It was Wisdom. His glory was even greater now, but He was again my size. *"Do you understand what happened just then?"* He asked.

Knowing very well that when the Lord asks a question He is not seeking information, I began to ponder what had happened. I knew it was reality. Compared to Him, I am less than a speck of dust would be to the earth, and for some reason He wanted me to experience that realization in a profound way.

Answering my thoughts, He elaborated:

"What you are thinking is true, but this comparison of man to God is not just in size. You began to experience the power of My Words. To be entrusted with My Words is to be entrusted with the power by which the universe is held together. I did not do this to make you feel small, but to help you understand the seriousness and the power of that with which you have been entrusted—the Word of God.

"In all of your endeavors, remember that the importance of a single Word from God to man is of more value than all of the treasures on earth. You must understand and teach My brethren to respect the value of My Word. As one who is called to carry My Words, you must also respect the value of your own words. Those who will carry the truth must be true."

Meeting the Evangelist

While hearing these words, I felt compelled to look up toward one of the thrones beside me. Immediately I saw a man I recognized. He had been a great evangelist when I was a child, and many felt that he had walked in more power than anyone since the early church. I had read about him and had listened to some of his recorded messages. It was hard not to be touched by his genuine humility and the obvious love he had for the Lord and people. Even so, I also felt that some of his teachings had gone seriously awry. I was surprised, but also relieved, to see him sitting on a great throne. I was captured by the humility and love that still exuded from him.

As I turned to ask the Lord if I could talk with this man, I could see how much the Lord loved him. However, the Lord motioned for me to continue walking and would not permit me to speak with the evangelist.

"I just wanted you to see him here," the Lord explained, *"and to understand the position that he has with Me. There is much for you to understand about him. He was a messenger to My last-day church, but the church could not hear him for reasons that you will understand in due time. He did fall into discouragement and delusion for a time, and his message was distorted. It must be recovered, as well as the parts that I have given to others which were also distorted."*

Knowing everything here happened in perfect timing with all I was meant to learn, I began to think about how seeing this man must be related to what we had just talked about—the potential of power to corrupt.

"Yes. There is great danger in walking in great power," the Lord responded. *"Many of My messengers have fallen subject to this danger, and that is part of the message they are to give to My last-day church. You must walk in My power, even much greater power than these experienced. But if you ever start to think the power is My endorsement of you or even of your message, you will open the door to the same delusion. The Holy Spirit is given to testify only of Me. If you are wise, like Paul, you will learn to have glory more in your weaknesses than in your strengths.*

"True faith is the true recognition of who I am. It is nothing more and nothing less. But you must always remember, even if you abide in My presence and see Me as I am, you can still fall if you turn from Me to look at yourself. That is how Lucifer fell. He dwelt in this room and beheld My glory and the glory of My Father. However, he began to look at himself more than he looked to Us. He then began to take pride in his position and power.

"Many of My servants who have been allowed to see My glory and be entrusted with My power have fallen in the same way as Lucifer. If you begin to think that it is because of your wisdom, your righteousness, or even your devotion to pure doctrine, you will stumble too."

Confidence

I knew this was as severe a warning as anything that I had been told here. I wanted to go back and fight in the last battle, but I was having serious questions about being able to do so without falling into the traps that now seemed to be everywhere. I looked back at the Lord. He was Wisdom, and I thought of how badly I needed to know Him as Wisdom when I returned.

"It is good for you to lose confidence in yourself. I cannot trust you with the powers of the age to come until you do. The more confidence you lose in yourself, the more power I will be able to trust you with, if…."

I waited a long time for the Lord to continue, but He didn't. Somehow I knew He wanted me to continue the sentence, but I did not know what to say. However, the more I looked at Him, the more confidence I felt. Finally I knew what to say.

"If I put my confidence in You," I added.

"Yes. You must have faith to do what you are called to do, but it must be faith in Me. It is not enough for you to just lose confidence in yourself. That only leads to insecurity if you do not fill the void with confidence in Me. That is how many of these men fell to their delusions.

"Many of these men and women were prophets. But some of them out of insecurity would not let men call them prophets. Yet that was not the truth because they were. False humility is also a deception. If the enemy could deceive them into thinking that they were not really prophets, he could also deceive them into thinking that they were greater prophets than they were just by nurturing their self-confidence. False humility will not cast out pride. It is just another form of self-centeredness, which the enemy has a right to exploit.

"All of your failures will be the result of this one thing: self-centeredness. The only way to be delivered from this is to walk in love. Love does not seek its own."

As I was thinking about all of this, a wonderful clarity began to come. I could see the whole experience from beginning to end, having as its focus a single, simple message. "How easily I am beguiled from the simplicity of devotion to You," I lamented.

The Smile of the Lord

The Lord stopped and looked at me with an expression I pray that I will never forget. He smiled. I did not want to abuse this opportunity, but I somehow felt when He smiled like that I could ask Him anything and He would give it to me. So I took the chance.

"Lord, when You said, 'Let there be light,' there was light. You prayed in John 17 that we would love You with the same love that the Father loved you with. Will You please say to me now, 'Let there be love in you' so that I will love You with the Father's love?"

He did not quit smiling, but rather put His arm around me like a friend. *"I already said that to you before the creation of the world when I called you. I have also said it to your brethren who will fight along with you in the last battle. You will know My Father's love for Me. It is a perfect love that will cast out all of your fears. This love will enable you to believe Me so you can do the works that I did, and even greater works, because I am with My Father. You will know His love for Me, and the works you will be given to do will glorify Me. Now, for your sake, I say again, 'Let there be My Father's love in you.'"*

I was overwhelmed with appreciation for this whole experience. "I love Your judgments," I said. I then started to turn and look back at the judgment seat, but the Lord stopped me.

"Don't look back. I am not there for you now; I am here. I will lead you from this room and on to your place in the battle, but you must not look back. You must see My judgment seat in your own heart because that is where it is now."

"Just like the Garden and like the treasures of salvation…," I thought to myself.

"Yes. Everything that I am doing, I am doing in your heart. That is where the living waters flow. That is where I am."

He gestured toward me, so I looked at myself, pulling back the cloak of humility. I was stunned by what I saw. My armor contained the same glory that surrounded Him. I quickly covered it again with my cloak.

"I also prayed to My Father on the night before My crucifixion that the glory I had with Him in the beginning would be with My people, so that you will be one. It is My glory that unifies. As you come together with others who love Me, My glory will be magnified. The more My glory is magnified by the joining of those who love Me, the more the world will know that I was sent by the Father. Now the world really will know that you are My disciples because you will love Me, and you will love each other."

As I kept looking at Him, my confidence continued to grow. It was like being washed on the inside. Soon I was feeling ready to do anything He asked.

Angelo

"There is still someone you must meet before you return to the battle," He said as we walked. I continued to be astonished by how much more glorious He had become than even a few minutes before.

"Every time you see Me with the eyes of your heart, your mind is renewed a little bit more," He proceeded to say. *"One day you will be able to abide in My presence continually. When you do that, all you have learned by My Spirit will be readily available to you, and I will be available to you."*

I could hear and understand everything He said, but I was so captured by His glory that I just had to ask Him, "Lord, why are You so much more glorious now than when You first appeared to me as Wisdom?"

"I have never changed, but you have. You are changed as you behold My glory with an unveiled face. The experiences you have had are removing the veils from your face so that you can see Me more clearly. Yet nothing removes them as quickly as when you behold My love."

He stopped and I then turned to look at those on the thrones next to us. We were still in the place where the highest kings were sitting. Then I recognized a man who was close by.

"Sir, I know you from somewhere, but I simply cannot remember where."

"You once saw me in a vision," he replied.

I immediately remembered and was shocked! "So you were a real person?"

"Yes," he replied.

I remembered the day when, as a young Christian, I had become frustrated with some issues in my life. I went out into the middle of a battlefield park near my apartment and determined that I would wait until the Lord spoke to me. As I sat reading my Bible, I was caught up into a vision, one of the first ones I ever had.

In the vision I saw a man who was zealously serving the Lord. He was continually witnessing to people, teaching the Bible, and visiting the sick to pray for them. He was very zealous for the Lord and had a genuine love for people. Then I saw another man, named Angelo, who was obviously a tramp or a homeless person. When a small kitten wandered onto his path, he started to kick it but restrained himself, though he still shoved it out of the way, rather harshly with his foot. Then the Lord asked me which of these men pleased Him the most.

"The first," I said without hesitating.

No, the second, " He responded, and began to tell me their stories.

He shared that the first man had been raised in a wonderful family, which had always known the Lord. He grew up in a thriving church and then attended one of the best Bible colleges in the country. He had been given one hundred portions of His love, but he was using only seventy-five.

The second man had been born deaf. He was abused and kept in a dark, cold attic until he was found by the authorities when he was eight years old. He had then been shifted from one institution to another, where the abuse continued. Finally, he was turned out onto the streets. The Lord had only given him three portions of His love to help him overcome all of this, but he had mustered every bit of it to fight the rage in his heart and keep from hurting the kitten.

I now looked at that man, a king sitting on a throne far more glorious than Solomon could have even imagined. Hosts of angels were arrayed about him, waiting to do his bidding. I turned to the Lord in awe. I still could not believe he was real, much less one of the great kings.

"Lord, please tell me the rest of his story," I begged.

"Of course, that is why we are here. Angelo was so faithful with the little I had given to him that I gave him three more portions of My love. He used all of that to quit stealing. He almost starved, but he refused to take anything that was not his. He bought his food with what he could make collecting bottles, and occasionally he found someone who would let him do yard work.

"Angelo could not hear, but he had learned to read, so I sent him a gospel tract. As he read it, the Spirit opened his heart, and he gave his life to Me. I again doubled the portions of My love to him, and he faithfully used all of them. He wanted to share Me with others, but he could not speak. Even though he lived in such poverty, he started spending over half of everything he made on gospel tracts to give out on street corners."

"How many did he lead to You?" I asked, thinking that it must have been multitudes for him to be sitting with the kings.

"One," the Lord answered. *"In order to encourage him, I let him lead a dying alcoholic to Me. It encouraged him so much that he would have stood on that corner for many more years just to bring another soul to repentance. But all of heaven was entreating Me to bring him here quickly, and I, too, wanted him to receive his reward."*

A Different Kind of Martyr

"But what did Angelo do to become a king here?" I asked.

"He was faithful with all that he was given. He overcame all until he became like Me, and he died a martyr."

"But what did he overcome, and how was he martyred?"

"He overcame the world with My love. Very few have overcome so much with so little. Many of My people dwell in homes with conveniences that kings would have envied just a century ago, yet they do not appreciate them. Angelo, on the other hand, would so appreciate even a cardboard box on a cold night that he would turn it into a glorious temple of My presence.

"Angelo began to love everyone and everything. He would rejoice more over an apple than some of My people do over a great feast. He was faithful with all that I gave him, even though it was not very much compared to what I gave others, including you. I showed him to you in a vision because you passed by him

many times. Once you even pointed him out to one of your friends and spoke of him."

"I did? What did I say?"

"You said, 'There is another one of those Elijahs who must have escaped from the bus station.' You said he was 'a religious nut' who was sent by the enemy to turn people off from the gospel."

This was the worst blow that I had yet suffered in this whole experience. I was more than shocked—I was appalled. I tried to remember the specific incident, but could not—simply because there were so many others like it. I had never had much compassion for filthy street preachers, considering them tools of Satan.

"I'm sorry, Lord. I'm really sorry."

"You are forgiven," He quickly responded. *"And you are right that there are many who try to preach the gospel on the streets for wrong or even perverted reasons. Even so, many are sincere, even if they are untrained and unlearned. You must not judge by appearances. There are as many true servants who look like he did as there are among the polished professionals in the great cathedrals and organizations that men have built in My name."*

He then motioned for me to look up at Angelo. When I had turned, he had descended the steps to his throne and was now right in front of me. Opening his arms, he gave me a great hug and kissed my forehead like a father. Love poured over me and through me until I felt that it would overload my nervous system. When he finally released me,

I was staggering as if I was drunk, but it was a wonderful feeling. It was love like I had never felt before.

"He could have imparted that to you on earth," the Lord continued. *"He had much to give to My people, but they would not come near him. Even My prophets avoided him. He grew in the faith by buying a Bible and a couple of books that he read over and over. He tried to go to churches, but he could not find one that would receive him. If they would have taken him in, they would have taken Me in. He was My knock upon their door."*

I was learning a new definition of grief. "How did he die?" I asked, remembering that he had been martyred. Based on what I had seen so far, I was half expecting that I somehow was even responsible for that.

"He froze to death trying to keep alive an old wino who had passed out in the cold."

The Unlikely Overcomer

As I looked at Angelo, I could not believe how hard my heart had been. Even so, I did not understand how dying in this way made him a martyr, which I thought was a title reserved for those who died because they would not compromise their testimony of the lordship of Christ.

"Lord, I know he is truly an overcomer," I remarked. "And it truly is warranted for him to be here. But are those who die in such a way actually considered martyrs?"

"Angelo was a martyr every day that he lived. He would only do enough for himself to stay alive, and he gladly sacrificed his life to save a needy friend. As Paul wrote to the Corinthians, even if you give your body to be burned, but do not have love,

it counts as nothing. But when you give yourself with love, it counts for much.

"Angelo died every day, because he did not live for himself, but for others. Even though he always considered himself the least of the saints, he was truly one of the greatest. As you have already learned, many of those who consider themselves the greatest, and are considered by others to be the greatest, end up being the least here. Angelo did not die for a doctrine, or even for his testimony, but he did die for Me."

"Lord, please help me to remember this. When I return, please do not let me forget what I am seeing here," I begged.

"That is why I am with you here, and I will be with you when you return. Wisdom is to see with My eyes and to not judge by appearances. I showed you Angelo in the vision so that you would recognize him when you passed him on the street. If you had shared with him the knowledge of his past that I had shown you in the vision, he would have given his life to Me then. You could have then discipled this great king and he would have had a great impact on My church.

"If My people would look at others the way I do, Angelo and many others like him would have been recognized. They would have been paraded into the greatest pulpits. My people would have come from the ends of the earth to sit at their feet, because by doing this they would have sat at My feet. They would have taught you to love and how to invest the gifts that I have given to you so that you could bear much more fruit."

I was so ashamed that I did not want to even look at the Lord, but finally I turned back to Him as I felt the pain driving me toward self-centeredness again. When I looked at Him, I was virtually blinded by His glory. It took a while, but gradually my eyes adjusted so that I could see Him.

"Remember that you are forgiven," He said. *"I am not showing you these things to condemn you, but to teach you. Always remember that compassion will remove the veils from your soul faster than anything else."*

As we began to walk again, Angelo entreated me, "Please remember my friends, the homeless. Many will love our Savior if someone will go to them."

His words had such power in them that I was too moved to answer, so I just nodded. I knew that those words were the decree of a great king and a great friend of the King of kings.

"Lord, will You help me to help the homeless?" I asked.

"I will help any who help them," He responded. *"When you love those whom I love, you will always know My help. You will be given the Helper by the measure of your love. You have asked many times for more of My anointing; that is how you will receive it. Love those whom I love. As you love them, you love Me. As you give to them, you have given to Me, and I will give more to you in return."*

Living Like a King

My mind drifted to my nice home and all the other possessions I had. I was not wealthy, yet I knew by earthly standards I lived much better than kings had lived just a century before. I had never felt guilty about it before, but I did now. Somehow it was a good feeling, but at the same time it did not feel right. Again I looked back to the Lord, for I knew He would help me.

"Remember what I said about how My perfect law of love made light and darkness distinct. When confusion such as you are now feeling comes, you know what you are experiencing is not My perfect law of love. I delight in giving My family good gifts, just as you do yours. I want you to enjoy them and appreciate them. Nevertheless, you must not worship them, and you must freely share them when I call you to.

"I could wave My hand and instantly remove all poverty from the earth. There will be a day of reckoning when the mountains and high places are brought down and the poor and oppressed are raised up, but I must do it. Human compassion is just as contrary to Me as human oppression. Human compassion is used as a substitute for the power of My cross. I have not called you to sacrifice, but to obey. Sometimes you will have to sacrifice in order to obey Me, but if your sacrifice is not done in obedience, it will separate us.

"You are guilty for the way you misjudged and treated this great king when he was My servant on earth. Do not judge anyone without inquiring of Me. You missed more of the encounters I set up for you than you have ever imagined, simply because you were not sensitive to Me. However, I did not show you this just to make you feel guilty, but rather to bring you to repentance so you will not continue to miss such opportunities.

"If you just react in guilt, you will begin to do things to compensate for your guilt, which is an affront to My cross. My cross alone can remove your guilt, and because I went to the

cross to remove your guilt, whatever is done in guilt is not done for Me.

"*I do not enjoy seeing men suffer,*" Wisdom continued. "*But human compassion will not lead them to the cross, which alone can relieve their real suffering. You missed Angelo because you were not walking in compassion. You will have more when you return, but your compassion must still be subject to My Spirit. Even I did not heal all those for whom I had compassion, but I only did what I saw My Father doing. You must not do things out of compassion, but in obedience to My Spirit. Only then will your compassion have the power of redemption.*

"*I have given you the gifts of My Spirit. You have known My anointing in your preaching and writing, but you have known it much less than you realize. Rarely do you truly see with My eyes or hear with My ears or understand with My heart. Without Me, you can do nothing that will benefit My kingdom or promote My gospel.*

"*You have fought in My battles, and you have even seen the top of My mountain. You have learned to shoot arrows of truth and hit the enemy. You have learned a little about using My sword. But remember, love is My greatest weapon. Love will never fail. Love will be the power that destroys the works of the devil, and love will be what brings My kingdom. Love is the banner over My army, and under this banner you must now fight.*"

With this, we turned into a corridor and were no longer in the great hall of judgment. The glory of Wisdom was all around me, but I could no longer see Him distinctly. Suddenly, I came to a door. My first impulse was to turn because I did not want to leave, but I knew that I must. This was the door Wisdom had led me to. I had to go through it.

To be continued....

 MorningStar Partners

T he most powerful spiritual force since the first century is mobilizing. We are looking at the greatest potential impact for the gospel ever seen. We need Partners to help raise up and send the most high-impact ministries in church history.

Join with us to equip the body of Christ through our schools, missions, conferences, television shows, and publications. Your contributions are used to train and equip all ages in their prophetic gifting. You can become a MorningStar Partner with a regular contribution of any amount, whether it is once a month or once a year.

Partnership Benefits:
- Receive monthly newsletters with rich, timely content from Rick Joyner and others
- Participate in live video webinars featuring key prophetic voices
- Connect with Partners and staff at exclusive Partner events and in our Koinonia Lounge
- Enjoy a complimentary subscription to the MorningStar Journal
- Save money with special discounts on products, hotel rooms, conferences, and more

Become a MorningStar Partner Today:

MStarPartners.org

or call
1-803-547-8495